Praise for *Crashproof*

"*Crashproof Your Kids* is in my opinion the best book available in the United States on safe driving. Although it has much to offer about best practices in driving techniques, it is also a lucid, well-structured and immensely praiseworthy approach to the single most vital aspect of good driving—*attitude.*"
—Eddie Wren, Vice President, Advanced Drivers of America

"I highly recommend ... ... ring supervised driving due to ... ... nd vehicle crashes. *Crashproof Your Kids* is a valuable resource, providing a template for parents to assist their teen driver develop safe driving skills and behaviors."
—Trish Johnson, VP of Training, Top Driver, Inc.

"*Crashproof Your Kids* is one of the best researched and thought-out books on teen driving available. It's exceptionally valuable, and will help parents keep their loved ones alive on the road."
—Gordon M. Booth, Chief Instructor, Drivetrain, Inc.

"As Timothy Smith points out, the number one killer of kids is not car *accidents,* but car *crashes. Crashes* are preventable. This life-saving book is required reading for the teen-driver families with whom I work. It should be required for all teen-driver families."
—Michael J. Bradley, Ed.D., author of *Yes, Your Teen Is Crazy!;*
Yes, Your Parents Are Crazy!; and *The Heart & Soul of the Next Generation*

"Before I got out of First Gear I had already gotten my money's worth. This easy-to-follow book guides you through a series of steps to help keep your teen alive on the road. Every parent of a teenager should have this book. Read it and Reap."
—Sam Horn, author of *Tongue Fu!®, What's Holding You Back?,*
and *POP! The Art and Science of Being One-of-a-Kind*

"*Crashproof Your Kids* is kid- and parent-friendly, with a great deal of good information. I especially like the rhymes to help remember the concepts."
—Debbie Cottonware, 2003 ADTSEA Driver Education Teacher of the Year

CRASH

FIRESIDE
Rockefeller Center
1230 Avenue of the Americas
New York, NY 10020

FIRESIDE and colophon are registered trademarks of Simon & Schuster, Inc.

Designed by Jamie Kerner-Scott

Manufactured in the United States of America

10   9   8   7   6   5   4   3   2   1

Library of Congress Cataloging-in-Publication Data is available.

ISBN-13: 978-0-7432-7711-2
ISBN-10:   0-7432-7711-2

For information regarding special discounts for bulk purchases, please contact Simon
& Schuster Special Sales at 1-800-456-6798 or business@simonandschuster.com.

PROOF
YOUR KIDS

Make Your Teen a Safer,
Smarter Driver

TIMOTHY C. SMITH

A Fireside Book
Published by Simon & Schuster
New York   London   Toronto   Sydney

Dedication

To all parents and their teenagers, may you have safe,
enjoyable journeys and meaningful destinations.
To Brittany, Nicholas, and Alexandra, may you drive
through life with skill, awareness, and joy.

Regret for the things we did can be tempered over time; it is regret for the things we did not do that is inconsolable.

Sidney J. Harris

CONTENTS

Third Gear: Increasing the Challenge

Fourth Gear: Reducing Risky Behaviors

Part 3: The Homestretch

FOREWORD

Not long ago, my community was torn apart by almost two dozen car crash fatalities. Most of those killed were young and vibrant teens, who at various times of the day and night, with and without alcohol as a factor, lost their lives as the result of getting into a car and hitting the road.

Their parents were, understandably, devastated. The community was shocked. Memorial markers seemed to be everywhere. Every teen driving news story had another sad ending. And, reliably, there was the sort of hand-wringing that follows these kinds of tragedies. Parents, legislators, community leaders—everyone wanted to know what to do. Like with most things, the answer has always been there.

Here's what we know—*parents make a difference.* A huge difference. As a parent, your approval is required for your young drivers to get their learner's permit and ultimately their license. If you want to keep your teens alive on the road today, you need to get—and STAY—actively involved. The more time you spend in the car with your teens, practicing good, solid driving skills, as well as coaching proper attitude, the better the chance they'll survive their teen years. Timothy Smith has created a formidable guidebook for the experience, finally giving parents the practical advice they need to create the kind of young drivers who understand what driving is all about—including the social responsibility.

Good luck on the journey you and your young driver will make—together!

Kristin Backstrom
President, Safe Smart Women

INTRODUCTION

Is there anything scarier to a parent than handing over the car keys to a teenager?

Remember what it was like when we got our licenses? We sat through classes that droned on about traffic regulations, watched some gruesome crash films, and spent a couple of hours driving with our fourth-period geography teacher. Then we got our licenses, and away we went.

That doesn't cut it anymore. Your teen faces far more dangers on the road than we did: snarled rush-hour traffic, road rage, multiple distractions, and increased mind-altering substances, just to name a few.

It's no wonder that the leading cause of death for teenagers today is not guns, suicide, or drugs. It's car crashes.

Consider these sobering statistics:

- 58 out of 100 new drivers get into a crash the first year.
- 16-year-olds are 20 times more likely than an adult to die in an automobile crash and 3 times more likely than an 18- or 19-year-old.
- Every single day, 19 people 15 to 20 years old are killed, and more than 1,800 are injured in vehicle crashes.

Notice that I did not use the word *accidents*. We're talking about *crashes*. An accident is when a meteor falls on your car. When your son bangs up your car because the guy in front of him stopped quickly or because the road was slippery, it's no accident. Car crashes are almost never accidents, and the distinction is an important one, because the vast majority of crashes are caused by driver error, and they're preventable.

I didn't originally intend to write a book on this subject. But within a six-month period, five teenagers were killed in three separate crashes near my home. I was further shocked to discover that nearly every teenager in my neighborhood had at least one crash within a year of getting his or her license. My oldest daughter was 14 and would soon be learning to drive, and my son and youngest daughter were right behind her, so I began looking for resources to help my kids become better, safer drivers.

I read every book, article, and publication on the subject that I could get my hands on and interviewed driving instructors, academics, psychologists, professional racers, paramedics, safety experts, parents, and teens. I completed several defensive-driving courses and became a certified driving instructor and a licensed racing-car driver.

The more I learned, the more dismayed I became. Although the auto industry has made significant progress with safety features, innovations in driver education have lagged. In many ways, the methods used to train young drivers today haven't improved much since Ward and June Cleaver sent the Beaver out onto Pleasant Lane. For the past several decades, we've given our teens an average of 30 hours of classroom study and 6 hours of behind-the-wheel training, and then we've done little but mourn the daily, weekly, and yearly toll the highways take on our youth.

Parents have the ultimate responsibility to ensure that their teenagers develop safe driving skills and behaviors. But too many, either underestimating their role or lacking effective methods, have failed to help equip their teens to handle the single most dangerous thing they will ever do, at their most risky age. The results of this lack of parental involvement have often been disastrous.

But here's the good news. Research has shown that the chances of a teen being involved in a crash can be reduced by up to *one-third* when parents take an active part in helping their teens learn to drive and set certain driving guidelines. And the heart of this book, the Crashproof Plan, takes you step by step through a series of driving exercises designed to make your teen a safer, smarter driver. It includes:

- Successful defensive-driving tactics and crash avoidance techniques.
- The most important advanced driving skills to teach your teen.
- How to deal with distractions, hazardous conditions, and drug and alcohol use.
- Strategies for communicating and working with your teen.
- A Crashproof Contract outlining expectations and responsibilities.

And there's much more.

The Crashproof Plan is not designed to replace the standard high school or commercial driver education curriculum. It doesn't deal with the most basic details of operating a car, such as how to drive with a stick-shift transmission. Instead, the Crashproof Plan begins where traditional driver education programs end, offering valuable information, anecdotes, and humor from experts as well as parents just like you. Standard driver education classes will teach your teen the basics of learning to drive. *Crashproof Your Kids* will help keep your teen alive.

You'll find this book essential if your teen:

- Will soon begin or is currently enrolled in a driver education program to obtain a permit or license.
- Has completed such a program and needs to fulfill a period of parental-supervised driving prior to obtaining a permit or license.
- Already has a permit or license and has been driving for some time, but you want to help increase his or her comfort, skill, and safety behind the wheel.

- Has already had a crash or a fender bender, and you want it to be the last one.

My daughter worked with me for more than a year to field-test the concepts embodied in the Crashproof Plan, as she progressed from permit to license to gradually more independent driving. Time will tell how well her crashproofing endures, but I sleep better knowing she has successfully completed this program.

The only thing you need to make this book work for you is the most precious gift you can give your teen: your time. And the return on that investment is priceless.

Every week, I hear or read about another terrible crash involving teenagers, most of them caused by momentary lapses, driver error, or bad judgment. If this book can help one family avoid a life cut short, with memories that will haunt them for years, it will have served its purpose. So let's get started.

Thank you for deciding to make a difference.

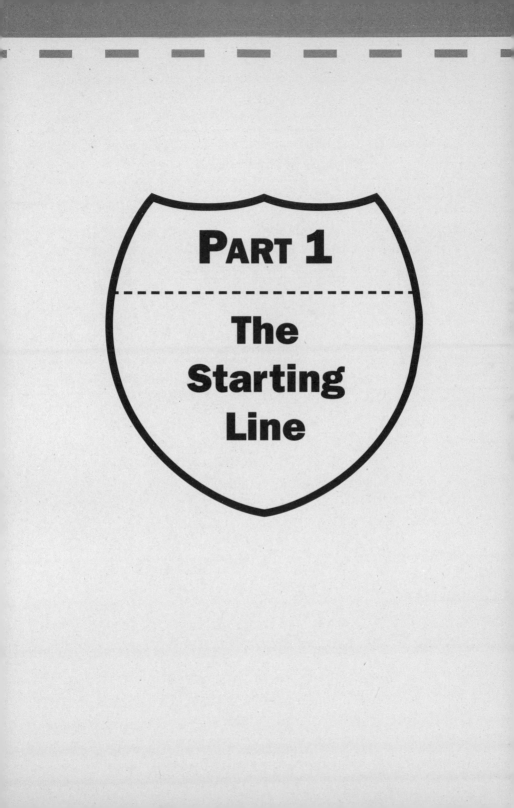

PART 1

The Starting Line

The Crashproof Plan Essentials

Fortune favors the prepared mind.
LOUIS PASTEUR

Here's what happens *in less than a second* when a car traveling 55 mph hits a stationary object:

- *0.1 second:* The front bumper and grille of the car collapse. If the car has an air bag, it has already inflated.
- *0.2 second:* The hood crumples, rises, and strikes the windshield as the rear wheels lift off the ground. The fender wraps around the struck object.
- *0.3 second:* The driver's legs jam under the dashboard and break, while the steering wheel heads for the driver's chest.
- *0.4 second:* The car's wrecked front end comes to a stop, but the car's rear is still rushing forward, and the driver's body is still traveling at 55 mph.
- *0.5 second:* If the car is not equipped with an air bag, the driver is smashed against the steering wheel, crushing arteries and lungs.
- *0.6 second:* The driver's feet are ripped out of their shoes. The brake pedal snaps off, and the car's frame buckles in the middle. Without an air bag, the driver's head smashes into the windshield.

• *0.7 second:* The passenger door rips loose, and the rear doors fly open. The front seat rams forward, pinning the driver further against the steering wheel shaft and dashboard, as the backseat breaks free and strikes the driver, who may already be dead.

Sometimes we need a jolting reminder of why effective driver training is so important and how shockingly fast lives can change forever.

We have a collective blind spot in North America when it comes to the importance of training teen drivers. The training requirements for driver licensure are much less comprehensive than for other, far less hazardous activities. Consider that in the state of Illinois, an apprentice plumber is required to put in a minimum of 1,500 to 1,600 hours of supervised training in the first year. To become a licensed journeyman plumber, someone will typically spend 6,400 hours of in-field training and 800 to 1,000 hours of classroom work over a four-year period.

Yet, with the possible exception of a cardiac arrest when a customer sees the bill, plumbers don't frequently kill or injure themselves or anyone else while fixing leaky pipes. It's clear that many of our training and licensure requirements are out of whack when compared to the risk factors associated with them.

Teen driver training requirements in the United States are also far less rigorous than in many other countries. In Germany, obtaining a driver's license is possible only after turning 18, completing 24 hours of class work, logging 20 hours of driving with a certified driving instructor, passing a rigorous test (which is failed by more than half the takers), and paying more than $2,000. Then you get a two-year probationary license.

More rigorous training has proven to pay off, too. In Australia, road safety organizations recommend at least 120 hours of parental-supervised driving, and Australian crash rates are substantially lower than in the United States. Swedish research indicates that teens with an average of 118 hours of supervised driving had 35 percent fewer crashes after licensure than those with an average of 44 hours of supervised experience. Sweden and Great Britain, which require comprehensive driver training, both have auto fatality rates less than half that of the United States.

Despite these facts, many parents assume that traditional driver education programs are sufficient and provide enough training to make a major impact on their teens' driving ability and future safety. They're dead wrong. With limited hours of classroom and behind-the-wheel time, only traffic regulations and the fundamentals of car control can be covered. We give our teens a handful of hours to learn traffic laws and drive with an instructor, and then we wonder why the injury and death rates are so high?

In addition, many high school driver education programs have been eliminated or have suffered substantial reductions in funding. The subsequent expansion of for-profit driver education schools has been distressingly haphazard, with little consistency in training, curriculum, and methods among the thousands of programs in this country.

Most programs have little time to focus on risk factors, defensive-driving skills, and accident avoidance—the very things that help keep our kids alive as they become better drivers. The other factors and pressures that have such an impact on driving behavior—social, parental, peer—are simply outside the scope and influence of driver education teachers.

It should be noted that many driver education teachers are skilled, caring individuals who do a job every day that most of us would need heavy sedation to do full-time. Their instruction is an essential first step in the learning process for teens. But it's only a first step. Far more time and effort are needed to develop safe, skillful drivers than is possible with the current level of resources dedicated to driver education programs.

While increased governmental and school spending on teen driver education would undoubtedly help, *the primary responsibility lies with us, as parents.* They're our kids and our precious heritage. And you have been granted clear authority: *no child under 18 in this country can obtain a learner's permit or a driver's license without a parent or legal guardian's written consent.*

The Crashproof Plan is part of the solution to increasing the effectiveness of teen driver training. It won't be a cakewalk if you do it right. You have years of ingrained driving habits, which may or may not be the best ones to impart to your teen. And, like many parents, you may have difficulty communicating with your teenager. (If you disagree with the last point, you are either exceptionally fortunate or perhaps slightly delusional.)

Your teen is not jumping up and down with joy at the thought of enduring a series of lectures from parents about driving, accompanied by that god-awful '70s and '80s music you listen to on the radio. Your son is pretty sure that within a couple of weeks, he will drive better than you do, and your daughter mostly wants you to give her the keys, let her social life blossom, and get the heck out of the way.

Finally, your calendar is jammed. You don't have big blocks of time to be allocated, no matter how worthy the cause.

Relax. You can do this. These are not insurmountable obstacles, and the Crashproof Plan is your secret weapon.

You don't have to be an experienced driving instructor to make the Crashproof Plan work. All it takes is time and proven methods. This book will provide the methods and break them down into manageable exercises that you can fit into a hectic schedule. If you think that there's just too much on your plate to do this, remind yourself of how valuable the investment will be for the well-being of your child and your family. Of all the things that compete for our attention, why wouldn't this be at the top of the list?

Consider for a moment all the time you already spend in service of your son or daughter. More than any other generation in history, we've added chauffeur to our parenting duties. We shuttle our kids back and forth to see friends; to take lessons in dance, piano, and Spanish; to attend games and practices for soccer, baseball, basketball, football, volleyball, softball, and tennis; and to parties, dances, meetings, and club functions. If we were paid chauffeur rates for all the running around we do for our kids, we'd all be retired and living in Fiji by now.

But teens don't die at soccer games and ballet practices. Take advantage of the time you might spend driving them back and forth by using it as part of your supervised driving time. Have your teen do the driving with you to his or her activities and to your regular circuit of the grocery store, pharmacy, and dry cleaner.

If you can find consistent days and times to set aside, you'll be much more likely to stick with the Crashproof Plan and make good progress. Sit down with your calendar and your teen's schedule, and plot out the time slots that will be the most available. Mark it on your calendar to reinforce the commitment. As competing events arise, treat the time you've set aside with the priority it deserves.

The prospect of reducing some of this burden by having our teens drive themselves to places as soon as they get their licenses can be compelling. Weigh those benefits very carefully, because crashes are actually most likely to occur in these local situations. Teens are more likely to be under time pressure, carry other passengers, and have their guard down a little on familiar streets. Shift the driving burden only as they prove ready, and be especially careful about additional distractions or weather hazards.

The purpose of the Crashproof Plan is to better the odds of teens surviving their driving, which too often ends up as a form of high-stakes gambling. Every time your teen gets behind the wheel, his or her hand of cards includes training, mood, car condition, weather, road hazards, and the behavior of other drivers.

The foundation of the Crashproof Plan rests on solid data, helping you determine the biggest payoffs for your time and effort, as well as suggesting how to work most effectively with your teenager. Some of the statistics leading to the creation of specific exercises support the conventional wisdom about teen drivers. Others may challenge your preconceptions and rearrange your priorities.

For example, the facts concerning what actually causes the most fatal crashes among young teen drivers are noteworthy. National publicity and awareness efforts have focused on teen drinking and driving, and rightfully so, but the percentage of fatal accidents involving teens and high blood alcohol is much lower than that of those caused by driver error. According to 1998 data released by the Insurance Institute for Highway Safety and the National Highway Traffic Safety Administration, *driver error* is by far the single biggest contributor to fatal accidents, responsible for more than 80 percent of crashes involving 16-year-olds. The good news is that driver errors are often easier to reduce than a teen's tendency to speed, carry multiple passengers, or use intoxicants.

No one can ever be truly *crashproof.* Complete immunity from all the variables that come into play in an automobile crash is not possible. But there is no question that you can help make your teen far more crashproof than he or she is now. Being crashproof means understanding both the nature of driving hazards and how to react with appropriate responses and strategies. Teens do not intuitively understand many of the threats involved in driving, and they have little experience in assessing which ones they are most likely to encounter and which ones are the most dangerous. Perceived risk differs from actual risk, and your teen needs help differentiating between the two.

That's where you come in, to educate and equip them to deal with the risks they will encounter on the road. The Crashproof Plan suggests a variety of ways to help you accomplish this and incorporates exercises intended to develop instinctive responses to hazardous situations.

The goal is not so much to preach or teach in the classic student/ teacher model as it is to give your teen a tangible, desired goal—

increasing freedom and the privilege of driving an automobile on his or her own—with the specific steps needed to achieve that goal.

One of the most effective methods that many states have found to reduce the toll of teen crashes and deaths is to mandate graduated driver licensing (GDL) programs. GDL programs treat driving as a kind of apprenticeship, where increasing freedom and privilege are earned through a phased-in system of driving situations. GDL began in the United States in Florida in 1996, and now virtually every state and Canada use some form of graduated licensing, which typically restricts beginning drivers from the riskiest situations as their experience and skill develop.

The best GDL programs include what studies have shown to be most effective in changing teen driving behavior: *specific instructions on skills, attitudes, and road etiquette, combined with adequate time and supervision, augmented by meaningful penalties and consequences.*

The Crashproof Plan provides a framework for you to integrate these important elements. Equipped with methods *proven* to reduce crashes and deaths significantly, you can create your own improved version of a graduated licensing program specifically for your teen.

Consisting of four "gears," the Crashproof Plan is designed to be a flexible outline and blueprint to help your teen develop skills in different situations and conditions by gradually increasing the levels of complexity, distraction, and challenge.

In First Gear, all road trips will take place during the daytime and in good weather and will focus solely on the operation and road feel of the automobile. Driving will be done at low speed and with minimal traffic. No additional distractions, such as radio, passengers, cell phones, food or beverages, should be allowed.

First Gear is an especially important part of the Crashproof Plan, because it's where you will determine a baseline for your teen's driving skill level and adjust the subsequent learning exercises accordingly. First Gear is also where you'll begin to establish your most comfortable methods of communicating and working together, ideally without wanting to strangle each other.

Once your teen is comfortable with operating a car in low-stress driving environments such as parking lots and residential streets, it's time to shift into Second Gear. In Second Gear, driving sessions will take place mostly in busy parking lots, on residential streets, and on country roads. These venues will provide the training ground for developing several important abilities essential for crashproofing: concentrated focus, increased awareness, and comprehensive visual scanning skills.

One of the primary goals in Second Gear is to further develop a defensive driving attitude, a mind-set that doesn't count on other drivers to obey laws and make good decisions consistently. Developing this "what if" mentality reinforces how quickly routine situations can turn nonroutine and stresses the importance of having an immediate action plan for making quick decisions. The longer driving sessions suggested in Second Gear help improve the ability to focus, and exercises devoted to space management, visual scanning, and increasing awareness all help guide where that focus should be directed.

Third Gear is where all the skills and experience built throughout the previous chapters get integrated, enabling the handling of higher speed, thicker traffic, and hazardous weather conditions. Strategies for freeway driving, negotiating the hustle and bustle of the city, and dealing with loss of vehicle control and mechanical failures will be covered.

Fourth Gear focuses on how to mitigate the most dangerous influences on your teen's driving behavior, with dozens of tips, strategies, and exercises designed to address distractions, disabling substances, road rage, and speeding. You'll be much more of an active observer during Fourth Gear, less of a show-and-tell teacher. This is where you mix up the locations, lengthen the driving times, and loosen the reins a little. If your teen has a license by now, you can build in solo driving time as he or she shows competence and confidence.

In the Homestretch, the final section of the book, the Crashproof Contract will help specify joint expectations and responsibilities involving use of the car and driving behavior. In addition, you'll find valuable information on advanced driving schools, selecting a vehicle, and a number of ways to keep track of your teen's driving.

If you follow all the sessions, you'll spend at least 50 hours with your teen in behind-the-wheel supervised driving. *In other words, a total commitment of one long work week to help establish a lifelong edge for your child.*

It's recommended that this time be spread out over at least a six-month period, to provide the minimum time necessary for the most important skills, principles, and attitude conditioning to be gradually learned and internalized. Committing yourself and your teen to a relatively lengthy training process also emphasizes its seriousness and ensures a variety of weather and driving conditions.

Consider helping your teen learn to drive a *gift of time,* as well as a situation in which there is undeniable incentive to spend time with you. It's a rare and fleeting opportunity to spend side-by-side quality time with our teens before they go off on their own into the world.

The fact that you've picked up this book means that you care enough to be actively involved with the single most dangerous thing your teenager will do while under your care. You want to make a difference, however you can. And you will, with some help to assist your teen in avoiding the most lethal dangers of the road.

The strategies and behind-the-wheel exercises in this book combined with your desire and active participation will make your teen a better, safer driver. It might even make *you* a better, safer driver in the process—which is no small benefit to your teen, by the way.

The lessons you teach as your teen learns to drive will serve as a metaphor for how he or she drives through life. Operating a car embodies many of the adult challenges a teen will soon face: assuming responsibility for expensive possessions, resisting multiple temptations, and developing the maturity to deal with frustrating situations. You've got a very short window in your teen's life to make a very big impact. Your challenge is to make this process instructive, without it degenerating into a series of confrontational episodes replete with eye rolling, shouting, or stony silences. This book will help you accomplish that, too.

I can't guarantee that your child will never be involved in an auto crash or promise that your relationship and communication will be forever improved as a result of this interaction. If I could, this book would cost the equivalent of a new Ferrari, rather than that of a movie ticket and a tub of popcorn.

What I believe to be a reasonable promise, however, is that by using this book in conjunction with focused driving sessions and sensible restrictions, you will substantially reduce the likelihood of your child becoming involved in a crash. At a minimum, you will visibly demonstrate love and earn respect for being involved to an unusual degree in this crucial learning process.

You will also increase the likelihood that your children will be similarly involved in their children's journey toward safer driving, so your investment will reverberate in successive generations of your family.

All of this will remain unacknowledged, of course. We're talking about teenagers, after all.

Perhaps most important to remember and let your teen know, however, is that all the words and exercises in this book are in service of a very simple yet profound sentiment. It takes only 12 words to express it: *I love you. I'm worried about you. I want you back tonight.*

THE CRASHPROOF PLAN SCHEDULE

	FIRST GEAR	SECOND GEAR	THIRD GEAR	FOURTH GEAR
DURATION	1 month	1–2 months	3–4 months	3–4 months
AVERAGE TIME PER SESSION	30–45 minutes	30–60 minutes	30–60 minutes	60–90 minutes
LOCATIONS	Empty parking lots; low-traffic residential streets	Busy parking lots; moderate-traffic streets, country roads	Freeways; divided highways; heavier-traffic streets	Busy urban streets; all other types
DISTRACTIONS	None	None	Radio	Radio, passengers
ADDITIONAL CHALLENGES	None	Light traffic; increased speed	Heavier Traffic; highway speed	Heavy traffic; highway speed; rain and night driving; fog; snow; ice

You Are the Role Model

Role modeling is the most basic responsibility of parents.
Parents are handing life's scripts to their children, scripts that
in all likelihood will be acted out for the rest of the children's lives.
STEPHEN R. COVEY

Did you ever stop to think that your teen assumes it's only natural to drive while simultaneously talking on the cell phone, changing the radio station, passing a car, and keeping up with a conversation in the backseat while sipping a cup of cappuccino? Can you blame her? That's how she often sees you drive.

For better or worse, you have already established an example for your teenager with your driving skills and behavior. You've been observed by your child from an early age. She is fully aware of whether you stay within posted speed limits and signal your turns. If you are rude to other drivers, she will gather that this is an acceptable way to deal with the everyday frustrations of driving.

More important, our kids are not just observing, they're actually following our behavior. Do you roll through stop signs? If so, your son or daughter will, too. A study by the Insurance Institute for Highway Safety proves the connection between the driving habits of parents and their teenagers. A sampling of the study's eye-opening statistics:

- Drivers between the ages of 18 and 21 whose parents had three or more traffic violations over the past five years were 38 percent more likely to have their own violations than teens whose parents had no violations.

- For every crash on the parent's record, there was a 7 percent increase in the teen's crash rate.
- For every traffic violation on the parent's record, there was a 13 percent increase in the teen's violations.

In light of these statistics, you may want to reexamine your own approach to driving as you establish your role as mentor to your teen. This is obviously easier said than done. If you have a long history of moving violations, you may have more daunting odds in your quest to crashproof your kids. But you're automatically ahead of the game by being concerned enough to make use of this resource.

Own up to your own strengths and liabilities as a driver. If you have trouble distinguishing these, your teen or spouse will have no problem helping you. But also remember that the past is the past. A very powerful and disarming approach is to address directly an area of your driving that is less than stellar and say, for instance: "I don't set a great example here. I know I can do better, even at my advanced and decrepit age. It's important enough that I don't want you to repeat my bad habits, OK? There are a lot of things I would be proud to have you emulate. This isn't one of them."

Kids appreciate such honesty and willingness to admit fault. You show them how much you care by wanting them to do better than you. It's even more effective if you show by your driving behavior that you can change. It's a small price to pay to help such important messages sink in.

Your timing is good, too, because much of what your teen has observed in your driving habits until now has probably been somewhat subconscious. Not anymore. While you are helping your teen learn the many rules, strategies, and courtesies of the road, he will be more attuned to your own driving behavior than ever before.

As they observe, keep in mind that it's incredibly deceptive to our teens to watch us operate an automobile. Driving seems so easy, so mindless. One of the most difficult concepts to get across to teens is the complexity and potential risks inherent in everyday driving. Even their goofiest friends get licenses, and driving a car can appear pretty safe and simple. They see their parents drive with seemingly scant attention paid to it—we talk to them, we listen to the radio, we eat, we drink, we use one hand or one knee to steer. How difficult can it be?

What they are seeing, of course, is decades' worth of driving experience. We all make hundreds of observations and decisions every time we drive that collectively get us safely to our destinations. And we make those observations and decisions silently, for the most part. If your teen could hear your thoughts while you're talking and driving, it might sound something like this:

"So, did you have fun at Jennifer's last night?" *I can't believe that guy just pulled out in front of me. Gotta brake enough to stay off his bumper and not get rear-ended by that yellow Corvette on my butt. Hey, semitruck, you're creeping over the center line. Move over! Thanks, that's better. OK, Miss, I see you—would you like to get in here? There's a signal, come on in. Uh-oh, state police. I'm a little over the limit, but staying with the flow of traffic, should be OK. They make me nervous even when I haven't done anything wrong.*

"Really? Then what did she say?" *Nine minutes before I'm late. Man, the brakes feel squishy. When's the last time I had them checked? When I replaced that tire at the Shell station in, what was that, August? This is the longest red light in the state, I swear. Need to signal a turn here, come to a complete stop. That Bronco just went right through the red light! That wasn't yellow, not even pink. Dead red. Living dangerously, man.*

"Oh, I see. Well, you know, don't let it bother you, OK? Maybe she's not really such a good friend, huh?" *Why is this thing sputtering? Bad gas? I knew I shouldn't have gotten the cheap stuff at that gas station. Sorry, guy, I just cut you off. I think I can make this light before it changes.*

"Well, I don't blame you. But sometimes you just have to let things settle for a while, you know?" *There's Main, right here, two blocks down and then look for parking. Do not open that door, blue Buick. Good move, good move. Since when has that street been one way? Nuts, I'm a block south of where I thought I was.*

"No, we can't stop there now. We're already running late. That cute little purse will be there another time, trust me." *Hey, are you leaving? Yes! A parking space not too far away. Now crank it in, that's it, perfectly placed between both cars, could not have been . . .*

"Huh? Right. Have fun. I'll pick you up in two hours, hon, OK?"

To help your teen sharpen her awareness, focus, and decision making, practice *crashproof commentary,* continuous verbal expression of what the driver is seeing and reacting to on the road. This exercise forces drivers to verbalize their perception of their driving environment, talking about what they see, what they anticipate, and what they will do.

There's actually a little science to this approach. It's a well-known tenet of learning theory that the more senses that are involved, the greater the likelihood of memory, because several different areas of the brain are being used.

Think of learning how to spell a word. If a teacher tells you how to spell *perfume,* you will retain that knowledge to some degree. If the teacher tells you and then writes it on the blackboard, the odds of you remembering it improve. For maximum impact, you would have a student hold a bottle of perfume with the letters spelling it in large print on the label, repeat the word and its spelling while sniffing it, and write down the spelling on paper. The student has just used touch, vision, hearing, smell, and speech, all in connection with the word. What you've actually done is reinforce and rewire the neural connections in the brain that aid memory. That student is unlikely to misspell *perfume* in the future.

With crashproof commentary, using speech to reinforce what their eyes are processing, you're reinforcing, refining, and rewiring important neural connections in small but valuable ways. Another part of the brain has been engaged, and by working to expand and improve both vision and response, you'll help improve your teen's subconscious scanning and reaction skills, as well as the ability to perform complex acts without thinking about them.

This will take some persistence, and your teen will have to be prodded, especially in the beginning, to verbalize all the seemingly mundane things she observes on the road and what she plans to do about them. She'll feel like a geek. It's bad enough to be seen driving with her parents, and now you want her to talk to herself as if she's lost her mind or something.

But persist, because it can be illuminating. Begin by demonstrating it yourself while driving, giving a running monologue about speed limits, road signs, upcoming traffic, potential hazards, and your driving responses based on what you are seeing and expressing. Then have your teen do the same for a revealing demonstration of your differences.

Crashproof commentary can give you an excellent snapshot of how well each skill is developing, as well as how your teen ranks the relative importance of what he sees. It's also a great way to incorporate the "what if" game and connect it to an escape path or defensive maneuver. For example:

"I'm following a blue Toyota. Speed limit's 45, but she's going 35 one minute and 55 the next. Looks as if she's using a cell phone—that's probably why. Better give her another second or two of following distance. About a half-mile ahead, there's an intersection where I'm going to turn left. Checking the mirrors—nobody's behind me now, but I'll check again when I signal.

"I see a red car a couple hundred yards ahead on the right, looking to turn out of a subdivision and onto my road. If it turns now, the Toyota in front of me will have to brake—gotta watch that. I've got at least four or five seconds' following distance between us, so I should have plenty of time to brake. What if, because of that big space between us, he pulls out right in front of me instead? I should have time to brake, but if he cuts it close, I've got an escape route on the right shoulder and also on the street he pulled out from, because it's clear behind him."

Take advantage of this time of heightened awareness. When you drive, get your teen in the passenger seat next to you, serving as your navigator and driving partner. Talk through all the driving decisions you make on the way to school or the mall, which may seem very mundane and self-evident to you but not necessarily to your teen. You'll surprise yourself and your teen by verbalizing all the various things your brain, feet, and hands instinctively do while navigating everyday roads, intersections, and parking lots. It will also force you to heighten your awareness, which is one of the key skills you want to sharpen in your teen.

Speaking of commentary, when you're driving with your teen, keep the focus of your conversation about driving—the road, other drivers, improving visual scan, and making the right decisions. That doesn't mean you shouldn't make small talk or catch up a bit on their personal lives. But every conversation you have that forces your teen to think, respond, and react to the conversation takes away from concentration on driving.

Even worse is to use your time together to nag. It's tempting. Your teen is captive, after all. She can't slam the door, walk away, or cover her ears and go, "Blah, blah, blah, blah." Save the talks about friends, clothes, curfew, and attitude for another time. Driving a car is a full-on multitask endeavor, and you want to make clear that it takes a nearly all-consuming focus to drive safely consistently. On the road, one momentary lapse of attention has frightening potential consequences.

If you are able to work in concert with a spouse or partner, crash-proofing can be even more effective. If two people are involved, the responsibility is shared, and it also enables your teen to take advantage of (or be driven further crazy by) both of your different styles and temperaments.

Divide your roles and the behind-the-wheel sessions to take advantage of each other's respective interests and comfort. One partner's strong suit may be a direct, no-nonsense, linear approach—A, then B, then C. The other may be more attuned to a teen's particular learning style or more able to bring out and soothe a teen's fears or concerns.

If you are easily unnerved in heavy urban traffic, have your partner take those sessions, and you focus on parking skills and driving in light traffic conditions. If your reaction to mistakes involves yelling and your partner's is patient support, take the lead in Third Gear or Fourth Gear, after many of the initial hair-raising mistakes have been worked out.

Style differences aside, it's critical that you work together and make certain that the basics of what you impart are as similar as possible. It's not helpful to a teen to have to choose between the father's opinion that a two-second following distance is plenty and a mother's insistence that it be at least four seconds. If you have significant differences, work out an acceptable compromise beforehand, and stick with it. The value of your teen hearing messages several times diminishes if the messages are contradictory. Good communication between the two of you prior to a driving session helps maintain the consistency of the information and the methods behind the Crashproof Plan.

If you are divorced or separated, it's even more essential that you coordinate your approach to teaching your teen to drive. Divide the responsibilities, and talk to each other about where you see problem areas and progress, to avoid having your efforts weakened by inconsistency or major disagreements. Talk with your teen about his experiences driving with your ex to ensure that you are not sending opposite messages. If you are, reconcile your differences. Don't add another area where he is forced to choose sides.

Set mutually agreed-upon ground rules, since these have such an impact on crash rates. One of you may feel strongly about limiting passengers, cell-phone use, and night driving. If the other negates this by allowing all of these, it not only adds more emotional baggage to your relationships, but it also adds significant risk for your child. Whether single or together, the best way to make sure you are on the same page with your teen is to jointly craft and sign a Crashproof Contract (see Chapter 28), which specifies your most important agreements with respect to driving behavior and use of the car.

To summarize, in order to crashproof your teen, you'll need to strip away the complexity of the driving experience that we take for granted and build it back one step at a time for an impatient teenager. That takes discipline. It means you'll have to monitor your own driving behavior, as well as impose restrictions and consequences that your teen would probably rather do without.

In other words, it means applying the essence of responsible parenthood to the single deadliest endeavor your kid will undertake while under your care.

So bring the speed down a bit, use your turn signals, and stifle the urge to scream at the guy in front of you. You're being watched.

CHAPTER 3

Teaming with Your Teen

The invention of the teenager was a mistake. Once you identify a period of life in which people get to stay out late but don't have to pay taxes—naturally, no one wants to live any other way.

JUDITH MARTIN (MISS MANNERS)

Before you begin teaming with your teen, ask yourself a fundamental and critical question: *Is my teen really ready to learn to drive?* Many parents don't even consider this an option. Their teens consider driving a right and a rite of passage. At 15 or 16, they expect a learner's permit or a driver's license. That doesn't mean they're ready. Although 16 may be sweet, it's not a magical number. There's no reason you can't or shouldn't delay your teen's obtaining a permit or license until you are convinced that he or she is ready. Some are ready at 14, some not until 17 or 18. A *USA Today*/CNN/Gallup Poll found that 61 percent of those polled thought 16-year-olds were too young to have a driver's license. More than half thought teens should be at least 18 to get a license.

Parents trying to decide whether and when their teens are ready should consider how strongly their teens exhibit the following traits:

- *Attention span and focus.* Safe driving requires concentrated attention and focus, combining both mental and physical skills. Attention deficit disorder does not mix well with operating a 4,000-pound vehicle at 60 mph.

- *Decisiveness.* Behind-the-wheel decisions must often be made quickly. Dithering is dangerous.
- *Patience.* Complex skills take time to acquire, and it takes patience to deal with unexpected delays, heavy traffic, and clueless drivers.
- *Emotional control.* Good driving decisions are hard to make if you're crying, yelling, paralyzed with fear, or red-faced with anger.

The above characteristics will help you determine how ready your teen is to drive, and perhaps whether he represents an above-average crash risk. Keep in mind that even though teens are far more likely to crash than older drivers, many teens are as safe or safer than the average 30-year-old driver. The problem is that little definitive data exists to identify risky drivers *before* they crash, but an Atlanta-based psychologist, Dr. Michael Cantor, has been working on just that.

Dr. Cantor contends that there is a fundamental mismatch between how fast we go and how aware we are. He's developed a four-minute online test designed to help determine whether your teen is at risk behind the wheel and why. Arrangements to take the test can be made by calling Waypoint Research at 404-982-0011, or visiting *www.waypointresearch.com.*

It's almost guaranteed that your teen will think he's ready before you do. If you do decide to delay things, let him get his protests and howlings of unfairness out of his system. Life isn't fair for any of us, and the best parents are often benign dictators. Your teen may not like it, but if it's in his best interest, it's not negotiable. It will undoubtedly make you temporarily unpopular. Sorry, it's your job.

That doesn't necessarily mean that your teen doesn't begin to drive at all until a time when you deem he's ready. It may simply mean that his ongoing driver education with you will take longer. Some teens are ready to learn but may not be ready to get behind the wheel. Give this teen plenty of time to observe you drive, emphasizing crashproof commentary. Load him up with resources and instruction until you both feel he's ready to operate the car himself. Other teens are ready to drive but not ready to learn. That's a different problem, and a much more difficult one.

If you're likely to delay your teen's driving privileges or licensure, start talking about it early on. Peer pressure becomes more intense as friends begin getting their licenses and driving. (This also applies to the issue of whether they get their own car.)

To ensure your teen's buy-in for the Crashproof Plan, you'll need to go another mile.

ESTABLISHING A JOINT COMMITMENT

What does your teen expect out of this? If you ask her how long she expects the parental-supervised driving period to last, she's likely to answer, "Until I get my license, of course."

To be successful in using the Crashproof Plan, set your teen's expectations right up front. She will be far more likely to go along with a plan if you lay it out in some detail and she agrees that it's rational. By setting the expectations early and clearly, you reduce her sense of unfairness or surprise. Explain why you're taking this whole driving thing so seriously, and let her know that you both ultimately want to accomplish the same thing: the privilege of using an automobile. She should understand and appreciate the intent and the process, even if she doesn't agree with all of it.

First, ask what she most wants to get out of her time together with you and what she is most interested in and concerned about. Share with her the plan you're thinking about, and get her opinions. She may be surprised at the length of time you expect to be involved in her learning to drive. Most teens assume that as soon as they are eligible for their license, the period of supervised driving with you will be over. Remind her that not only is it a parental responsibility, but in most cases there is also a legal obligation for parental-supervised driving, at least before the license is obtained. How much supervised driving she needs after receiving a license is up to you, but in most of the United States, a minimum of 30 to 50 hours of parental-supervised driving is now required before a license can be obtained. For a full listing of state-by-state requirements for parental supervision and other restrictions, see the Appendix.

If where you live requires a graduated licensing process and a significant requirement for parental-supervised driving, tell your teen that she's worth far more than this barely adequate minimum.

If you live where little or no supervised driving is required, the rationale is even more powerful: you have no intention of waiting until some bureaucrat decides that it might be a good idea if fewer teens got killed on the highway. You're taking it into your own hands, with good data and great reasons.

Make it clear that supervised driving will phase out or end only when you feel your teen is ready. Let your teen know that your objective is to make sure that *you* are comfortable with each skill and experience level your teen attains. This is *your* responsibility, as a parent.

Explain your reasoning to your teen by citing the following factors:

1. Safe driving results from accumulated skills and experience. You are not going to short her on that. It's way too important.
2. A permit or license gives her permission to drive under specific conditions and restrictions, with a parent's written consent. It doesn't dictate how you will choose to be a parent to your teen, especially with respect to the single most dangerous thing she will be doing for the next several years. Her permit or license is the beginning of your involvement, not the end.
3. This will take a minimum of six months, more likely at least a

year. During this time, she will spend less and less time under supervision and be given more and more freedom and autonomy, as she earns it.

4. You want her to get her license and realize the freedom as well as the responsibility it entails, and together you'll create and work through a plan to make it happen.

5. Her involvement, opinions, and commitment are important, and you'll adjust to her needs and be practical and reasonably flexible. But the program itself isn't negotiable. And it won't change because she doesn't like it or because Heather's parents aren't making Heather do this.

If you're both ready to go, take a deep breath. Then think hard about your teen's personality.

Is she quick to react and physically and emotionally expressive? Or is she more laid-back, quiet, and even timid? Each teenager brings her own unique mind-set to operating an automobile. It's critical that you honestly assess her personality and behavioral traits, since these influence to a great degree what kind of a driver she'll be and how she conducts herself on the road. An aggressive teen with a quick temper will need your help to lessen those tendencies on the road. A spacey or indecisive teen will need your help in maintaining the mental focus essential for safe driving. It's both of your jobs to understand and mitigate the behaviors that can be most dangerous in driving circumstances.

Understanding and working with your teen's distinctive personality is especially critical for crashproofing, because although driver skills are important, they are only part of the equation. Several studies have shown that the choices made by drivers have more influence on safety than their skill in handling difficult road situations. While many continue to regard skill development as the most important feature of the driving experience, driver skill alone does not appear to lead to significant and long-lasting reductions in crash rates and overall safety. The choices your teen will make when it comes to wearing a seat belt, speeding, tailgating, accepting multiple distractions in the car, and using alcohol and drugs are even more important. In other words, you've got to concentrate not only on improving driving skills but also on the perceptions, motivations, and attitudes affecting your teen's behavior behind the wheel.

LEARNING PREFERENCE

How does your teen like to learn new things? Does he gobble up information quickly and in big chunks? Or does he prefer to digest it more slowly, processing new information bit by bit?

Does your teen prefer to be instructed or to read and learn for himself? This will determine the degree to which you assume the traditional teacher role or instead become more of a supervisor and provider of resources such as this book. One of the benefits of behind-the-wheel exercises is that when you are side-by-side having a conversation, it feels less like a lecture than when you're talking or instructing face-to-face.

Is he a patient and detail-oriented learner or more impatient, preferring just enough instruction to get to the action part? If the former, you'll do well to map out and present each step of the Crashproof Plan as it unfolds, providing lots of background and detail. If the latter, concentrate on the bullet points and the headlines, sprinkling in the details while he's actively *doing stuff*.

Has it always been important for him to have his progress measured and acknowledged? If so, spend more time after each driving session reviewing what has been learned and the progress you've seen, and give lots of positive feedback for his efforts.

For "right-brain" analytics, where an ordered procession of details leads to the best conceptual understanding, the step-by-step sequential format of the Crashproof Plan may work well with little modification.

If your teen is more left-brained, he may prefer to process many different general concepts simultaneously before digging into the details.

Does your teen learn best with visual or oral help? This may be an area where you are less likely to know with confidence which is preferred, so ask and then deliver. If your teen prefers listening to process information and likes to be told how to do things, emphasize a "tell me" approach. Spend more time describing exercises in detail, and talk about choosing the right responses to different driving situations.

If you are frequently asked to "show me," your teen is probably more visually oriented. He wants to see it in order to *replicate* it. The majority of people have been found to learn more information from visual perception than from auditory, which would suggest a "show rather than tell" approach to teaching. With this learning style, use more pictures and diagrams, and physically demonstrate the things you want to be learned.

An exciting new area of neuroscience adds further importance to visual learning. A cluster of neurons called "mirror neurons," which scientists have only recently discovered, appear to have a profound influence on what we feel and how we learn. Apparently, many of the same neurons fire in our brains when we watch someone do something as when we actually do the same thing. In other words, if you could trace the sequence of neurons firing in your brain that preceded your stepping on the gas and turning the wheel, they would match the sequence of somebody observing you do that. As observers, our brains are in effect going through the motions without our bodies actually doing it yet. Your teen's brain is unconsciously rehearsing the actions he may need to take by watching you do it. That also helps explain the power of example and how much our actions and behavior affect those who watch us the most closely: our kids.

The ultimate goal of teaching safe, effective driving behavior is to get that behavior hardwired, committed to long-term and instinctive memory. Our brains receive so much information and stimuli every minute that we consciously and unconsciously dump most of it shortly after we receive it. Some of it gets committed to short-term memory. You want to get the most important concepts and behaviors committed to your teen's long-term memory. To do that requires repetition and the incorporation of as many different senses as possible.

Cater to your teen's preferred modes of learning, and bear in mind that effectiveness increases if watching is combined with doing, and retention is better if more than one sense is involved. Your teen is much more likely to do exactly what he should do in a given circumstance without thinking if he's heard it and spoken it (which reinforces hearing it) and can actively visualize the correct sequence as he thinks or talks about it. His brain can't help but remember.

In addition to finding the methods that work best for delivering your information, you can also add more lasting impact by presenting it as more allegory than lecture. A good example is the whole idea that driving an automobile should be viewed as part of "driving through life." You can reinforce this in many ways, such as giving him tips on how to deal with road rage. But those same strategies are applicable elsewhere, because in essence they are how we respond to stressful situations with other people. Giving a stranger who's just annoyed you the benefit of the doubt and a little forgiveness pays off in more ways than just that particular driving episode. It has to do with the ability to control emotions, the empathy needed to recognize and pardon faults in others (and ourselves), and the will to deal with it as constructively as we can.

RESPONSE TO STRESSFUL SITUATIONS

When a deer runs out in front of you, a decision needs to be made *right now.* Brake? Swerve? Freeze? Driving a car can present stressful and challenging situations at any given time. Your teen will react to them much as she reacts to other stressful, challenging situations. She must understand that she has ultimate control of the decisions when driving and can't simply choose not to get involved. Indecision or poor decisions can be very costly, if not deadly.

Teens who naturally shy away from being decisive in challenging circumstances need to develop decisiveness for their encounters while piloting an automobile, and you'll need to help yours methodically build up confidence and nerve. You may want to wait several additional months before you have her tackle night driving on a busy highway, for example. Even more important is to practice appropriate driving responses over and over until she doesn't feel as if she has to agonize over a decision—it's become instinctive.

If your teen reacts to stress with a head-on and aggressive stance, make sure she understands the potential consequences of such an approach on the road. Your teen *will* be cut off by other drivers. Flipping them the finger or tailgating in retaliation can result in unpredictable and potentially nasty situations. Your teen *will* face the sudden oncoming headlights of other drivers when she pulls into the passing lane. Whether she speeds up to complete the pass or brakes and returns to her lane may be a life-or-death decision.

As her driving mentor, you can not only encourage safe behavior but also help in ways that take into account her particular needs and personality. If you tend to be confident and aggressive, you might well decide to speed up and complete that pass. Encouraging a much more passive and less confident son or daughter to do the same in that situation could be counterproductive, if not traumatic.

REACTION TO CRITICISM

Remember that your presence in the car as he learns to drive adds stress. Your teen wants to do well and to please you. He feels you watching and frequently commenting on his every move, so it's important that you be careful with your criticism. When you observe some-

thing that needs corrective action and are about to offer constructive criticism, first ask him what he thought about the driving maneuver that just happened. If he accurately points out what could have
been improved, you don't need to repeat it. If he doesn't, first point out
one or two things that he did well, and then get to the part that needs
fixing.

I found that I initially had difficulty giving constructive criticism to
my daughter. One of my strengths as a coach and teacher is in being direct and specific, focused on areas needing improvement. One of my
weaknesses is in not giving equal focus and acknowledgment to the
stuff that's being done well. That style works great for some and not so
great for others. My daughter's first reaction was to get defensive and
immediately argue about the advice, feeling that her driving skills were
being attacked. After a while, I got better at complimenting the things
she did well, and she got less defensive.

One way to defuse defensiveness and sensitivity to criticism is to let
your teen periodically get a shot at you. You be the driver, and have your
teen be the observer and teacher. Reversing roles gives your teen a
chance to show you how much he's grown in terms of awareness and
ability to make the right driving decisions, with the added benefit of
being able to make sure you're on the ball, too. It also provides a lesson
for both of you in giving constructive criticism. Your sensitivity to giving it can be sharpened by being on the other end of it.

Some of the benefits of driving a mile in their shoes:

1. It will give your teen a chance to observe and make comments
about your driving, which will make him feel good because the tables
are turned. He'll probably mock you a little, too, exaggerating the type
and tone of the comments you give him that annoy him the most. This
is great feedback, and you can acknowledge it, laugh at yourself, and
perhaps even change your style because of it. Give your teen a chance to
help crashproof *you.*

2. Your teen will have a chance to show that he has learned to pay at-

tention not only to good driving technique and behavior but also to the driving environment. He'll demonstrate it by what he says to you.

3. You'll focus on your own driving habits and how well you actually practice what you've been preaching.

4. Your teen might even gain a little empathy for what you're trying to accomplish, which in and of itself makes doing it worthwhile.

To help you realize these benefits, "driving in their shoes" sections are included in each of the four "Gears" ahead.

APPETITE FOR RISK TAKING

Your teen has already exhibited an appetite, or lack thereof, for taking risks. Count on her general approach to risk to carry over to her approach to driving. If she started climbing trees at three, skateboarding at five, and competitive motocross at eight, you will have more challenges in discouraging risky driving than with a teen more interested in chess, reading, and bird-watching. The setting of limits, earning and loss of privileges, and the severity of consequences for violating mutually agreed-upon rules may need to be different for the former and the latter teen.

Be aware of other types of potentially risky behavior you've observed in your teen. Does she get angry quickly, or has she ever gotten in trouble with her mouth? Have there been many occasions where she has acted impulsively in order to prove herself to someone or to exact revenge?

For the risk-averse teen, you may have to help develop more decisive (and, in her view, risky) driving behavior as she becomes more comfortable behind the wheel. Merging into heavy traffic, for example, can be problematic without a degree of decisiveness. We've all seen nervous drivers slow to a crawl or even a complete stop on merge ramps, causing a dangerous backup of cars accelerating behind them. For timid types, try a more gradual learning process broken down into several steps.

To teach her to merge into heavy traffic on a busy highway, for instance, try the following sequence:

- Map out on a piece of paper how a successful merge should happen, and talk through it. Then show how you could end up at the end of the ramp with no gap to merge into, and diagram the right way to pull off onto the shoulder and get back onto the highway when a gap appears.
- Next, you drive and demonstrate a successful merge, talking through it the whole way. Get off at the next exit, get back onto the highway, and, if you can do so safely, begin another merge, and abort it safely, pulling off onto the shoulder.

Now your teen can attempt it, having seen on paper and watched in person not only how it should go but also what to do if a problem is encountered. You've reduced most of the elements of fear and uncertainty through those exercises. Start by having her practice merging at the least busy time on the least busy stretch of highway. As her comfort and competence increase, have her practice merging in heavier traffic. Exercises similar to this are detailed throughout the Crashproof Plan.

GENDER

Does gender affect fender benders? At the risk of reinforcing gender stereotypes, some truisms about different driving behavior between males and females bear consideration. They have the weakness and strength of any such generalizations and may not be politically correct, but most are supported by some data and are consistently mentioned by parents, teachers, teens, and instructors. If you or your teen is an exception to any of these generalizations, that's wonderful. The world needs more exceptional people.

We all know through experience that boys and girls tend to communicate differently. A 2004 study by Cambridge University researched mothers and teenage daughters and the nature of their arguments. They found that bickering between mothers and their teenage daughters may actually signal a healthy relationship rather than cause for concern. Their evidence indicated that teenage daughters often start arguments to convey updated information about their interests and capabilities. But mothers often viewed the arguments as a form of rejection, tending to escalate the conflict. The girls' most frequent complaints were that their mothers didn't give them credit for being able to take responsibility, make good judgments, and understand the consequences of their actions.

The researchers suggested that the arguments be interpreted as an opportunity to get to know each other better. They noted in a news release: "The research suggests that both mothers and daughters can gain from the opportunity that arguing provides. For mothers particularly, recognizing the positive purpose of the inevitable quarrels may ease the daily tensions."

Taking this advice to heart, the following exchange can be envisioned:

"Mom, Audrey invited me to a party at Mike's house tonight. I told her I could take your car and drive her, Julie, Kara, and Sheena over there. We should be back around midnight."

"I don't think so. First of all, it's a school night. Second, you know you can't drive with multiple passengers. Finally, you know how I feel about Mike. Will there be any parents there?"

"You just don't trust me! You never let me go anywhere. My friends all think I'm a freak, and you treat me like a ten-year-old. I already told them I'd pick them up at eight. You can't do this to me!"

"Honey, I'm glad you've got several girlfriends you care about, and I appreciate you conveying to me updated information about your interests and capabilities. I know you're responsible, make good judgments, and understand the consequences of your actions."

"You do?"

"Yes. Absolutely."

"Great! Then I can go?"

"Heavens, no. It's a school night, you know you can't drive with multiple passengers, and you know how I feel about Mike."

Teenage boys, on the other hand, often communicate in a shorthand language consisting almost entirely of grunts. They won't bicker to convey information. That takes too much effort. So we learn, like mastering a new language, to interpret the grunts. The following is a near-verbatim conversation between my son and my wife.

"So, Nick, how was school today?"

"Nunh."

"Oh. Not so good on the geometry test?"

"Snork. Hnnh."

"You'll do better on the next one. What else is going on?"

"Yunf. Rwof."

"I can't believe Ashley said that."

"Urghh."

"Well, you've got to tell her that it bothers you when she does that."

"Euww. Arghh."

"I'm serious. Also—you're going to need to spend at least an hour on math homework tonight."

"Unhh. Rrrhh?"

"No way. And no video games until after your homework is finished."

Parents may need to work a little harder to communicate in full sentences with their sons.

You don't have to have long conversations with young males to notice that they tend to pay more attention to and take more pride in knowing how a car works and in their ability to "handle" a vehicle. This is reinforced by an automotive culture that is overwhelmingly dominated by males, who make up the vast majority of engineers, designers, executives, truck drivers, mechanics, collectors, enthusiasts, and professional racers.

This isn't a particularly good thing for young men learning to drive. The tendency of boys to define being a good driver as possessing good handling skills can lead to the riskier driving behavior exhibited by many male teenagers. They may feel more compelled to show off their skill, demonstrate a lack of fear in speeding, and push the envelope of a curve they have never negotiated.

Men teaching boys to drive need to be cautious about a double standard in tolerating a son's potential aggressive tendencies and "boys will be boys" horseplay. Males are much more frequent perpetrators and victims of road-rage incidents. Emphasize that you will judge him to be a good driver equally as much by how he treats other drivers and observes the rules and regulations of the road.

Use the skills boys may develop in video games—rapid hand-eye coordination and incorporation of multiple visual stimuli—and connect them to scanning and road-awareness exercises. Make it a competition to see how well he can see, process, and react appropriately to road situations, making multiple observations and decisions while maintaining focus on the immediate demands of the road ahead.

Keep two very important things in mind:

1. Males are more than twice as likely to die in automobile accidents than females.

2. Male passengers often equate to a testosterone turbocharge and significantly increase the risk, no matter who is driving.

Females more often define a good driver as one who has complete knowledge of the rules of the road and who operates the car in the manner in which they were taught. Crashes involving women have been shown to occur more frequently at intersections and at lower speed, on weekdays, and without alcohol involvement. Given their proportionately greater involvement in crashes at intersections, reiterate with girls that many people do *not* stop, do *not* observe the proper right-of-way, and generally may put them at risk. It may not be fair, and it certainly isn't right, but that's not the point. The point is that they need to be vigilant in situations where they may have a statistically higher likelihood of crashing—during the day, during the week, and at intersections.

Practice left-hand turns across traffic repeatedly with your daughter. Make sure she observes the two-to-three-second hesitation at lights and stop signs that will buy her an additional margin of safety. If she is not a video-game enthusiast, help her improve her ability to process multiple stimuli and make decisions and responses quickly.

Parents teaching girls would do well to talk more in their language—feelings, reactions, fears—without dismissing them or instinctively providing a fix. Much of the time, girls don't need a specific fix as much as they need you to empathize—to listen uncritically and let them know that you understand. Even if you can't relate to how they feel or you think they're wrong.

Some driving instructors believe that opposite-sex pairings often work better than same-sex pairings for teaching teens to drive. Father/daughter and mother/son pairings can often take advantage of different and complementary skill sets without reinforcing like-sex tendencies.

Both sexes can be susceptible to the distractions of music, passengers, and phones, with driving being considered part of a traveling social experience. Stress that they are the pilot first and foremost. Teens who are driving should not be equal participants in the car talk, engage in any cell-phone conversations, or fiddle with the radio while driving. They're the designated driver, and their one and only goal as such is to deliver themselves and their friends safely to their destination.

A final word about gender: throughout this book, I alternate between *he* and *she* when referring to your teen. All of the advice, information, and driving exercises are, of course, equally applicable for both sexes.

THE JEKYLL AND HYDE SYNDROME

As parents of teenagers, we're already painfully aware of their ability to change their personality overnight—or sometimes in the course of half an hour—depending on hormonal fluctuations and the incredibly annoying things we do to trigger their bizarre behavioral changes. Recent research indicates that there really is a biological basis for this behavior.

Dr. Jay Giedd, chief of brain imaging in the child psychiatry branch at the National Institute of Mental Health, has spent more than 14 years peering inside the heads of nearly 2,000 kids using magnetic resonance imaging (MRI). Giedd's studies have shown that extensive structural changes occur in adolescent brains for many years, probably until about age 25. Remarkably, age 25 is exactly when the crash rates for adults flatten out and stay relatively similar through the rest of adulthood. (It's also the age in most states when you can first rent a car, demonstrating that the rental-car companies, with cold, efficient clarity, have got it right.)

Apparently, the prefrontal cortex—the part of the brain primarily responsible for dealing with impulses and the consequences of actions—is the last part of the brain to mature, and your teen will be out of college before it does. Much otherwise inexplicable teen behavior is now thought to be caused by the lag in development between the rest of the brain and the part that helps them exercise judgment. Temple University psychologist Laurence Steinberg once said, in a quote especially well suited for this book, "It's like turning on the engine of a car without a skilled driver at the wheel."

As Claudia Wallis put it in her 2004 *Time* magazine article "What Makes Teens Tick?" "Now that MRI studies have cracked open a window on the developing brain, other researches are looking at how the newly detected physiological changes might account for the adolescent behaviors so familiar to parents: emotional outburst, reckless risk taking and rule breaking, and the impassioned pursuit of sex, drugs and rock 'n' roll."

Every day, they really are getting smarter but at the same time more confused, as their gray matter sparks like an overcharged battery. Do not under any circumstances make them aware of this emerging research. It'll only give them an excuse: "I couldn't help it, Dad. I had a really intense synaptic explosion last night. No way would I have rolled your car unless that happened. The nerves made me do it."

Adjust your mentoring style to the specific personality style your teen is exhibiting that day. And if sparks or smoke appear to be coming from the top of his head, it may not be because he's steamed at you. His brain may be on fire.

CHAPTER 4

A Dozen Reminders before You Buckle Up

Your children need your presence more than your presents.
JESSE JACKSON

Now you've got buy-in from your teen. (Or at least you've got grumbling acceptance that she understands what the program will be like.)

Before you get behind the wheel with your teen, consider the following twelve reminders.

1. He's nervous.

Driving can be challenging and sometimes a little intimidating. He also wants your approval, so he's going to be nervous. Make him feel at ease, and be gentle with your corrections, suggestions, and reprimands. Humor is always helpful, especially if it's at your own expense. Now would be a good time to tell him about that big hole you ripped in the side of your parents' car the first time you got to use it for a date.

2. Avoid making your trips together seem like lessons or nag sessions.

Some teens respond well to a structured approach. If yours does, use it. Tell her before you start that day's drive exactly what you want to accomplish and where and how you're going to accomplish it.

With many, however, your effectiveness will be enhanced if your teen is feeling as if you're just kind of riding along, but meanwhile you have a very clear sense of what you want to accomplish. You've deliberately chosen the setting, the key lessons, the specific exercises, and the postlesson analysis and goals. It just didn't seem so overt while you were doing it. This approach makes many teens feel less as if they're being constantly tested. They get plenty of that in high school.

Remember also that you have a captive audience. Resist the temptation to bring along other baggage unrelated to their learning to drive or to catch up on your nagging. She gets plenty of that at home.

3. Tone it down.

If you tend to get excitable or yell at your teen when he makes mistakes, keep in mind what such a reaction might cause while he's handling a vehicle. Grit your teeth, breathe deeply, and work to develop the kind of voice that the best driving instructors possess: calming, rational, and unruffled.

If you have a spouse or partner working with you in helping your teen learn to drive, talk about each other's respective strengths and weaknesses in communicating with your teen, and design a game plan that takes them into account. If you have any questions about what those strengths and weaknesses are, your spouse will have no problem helping you identify them.

4. She's listening.

Just because it seems as if she's blowing you off doesn't mean she's not hearing you. It's part of a teenager's job to be contrary for the sheer joy of contrariness. Sighs, complaints, and eye rolling mean she's listening. Your teen needs and wants to know what you think, to fine-tune her sense of what's right and wrong, and to better understand what's safe and what's dangerous.

What you should worry about is a total lack of reaction. That probably means she's tuning you out and thinking about what to wear for tonight's date, which she hasn't, by the way, told you about yet.

Stay on message, and don't be afraid of repetition. Her brain needs it for long-term memory. It's normal for her to resist what you're saying, if only to see how serious you are about it. Just make sure you've got a solid basis for what you're telling her.

5. Use the corny phrases.

It will be a challenge for your teen to absorb and remember everything you'll be trying to impart. Memory aids are always helpful, so sprinkled throughout this book are handy rhyming sayings which are guaranteed to help teens remember important concepts as well as cause their eyes to roll back in their heads.

I prefer to believe that when teenagers' eyes roll back in their heads, it triggers a neural pathway in their brains that leads to memory. At a minimum, it will add to the store of stupid stuff their parents say that they can regale their friends with. But the amazing thing is that much of this stuff will stick, sort of like when a song gets lodged in your head and you can't get rid of it. The point is, memory is enhanced when vivid images or words connect to a concept. Ten years from now, it's unlikely your teen will remember the hydrodynamic principles that cause a car to hydroplane, but just before she hits the cruise-control button as it starts to rain, she may well remember "Cruise in the rain, bruise on the brain." Twenty years from now, when she's helping her own teens to drive, she'll hear herself say, "To stay out of trouble, protect your bubble," and immediately thereafter will sigh, "Shoot me, please. I'm turning into my mother."

Make up your own phrases, if you like, but make an effort to stimulate memory. Maybe offer the incentive that you will promise not to use the sayings as soon as he demonstrates you don't need to.

6. This is a special and unusual time.

How rare is it to have your teen motivated to do something with you? OK, maybe a lot of that motivation has to do with obtaining a new way to get away from you, preferably in your car. But sitting side-by-side and working toward a shared goal is a pretty rare thing for parents and teenagers. Think of it this way: you've got hours of time to spend together where none of the conversation revolves around curfew, clothes, or calculus. And unlike with calculus, you've actually got some helpful information.

For dads and daughters in particular, this can be valuable. Dads often find it harder and harder to communicate with their daughters as they reach their teen years. Their daughters are often much more comfortable talking to their mothers about their changing bodies, their nasty but inseparable girlfriends, and their insensitive but longed-for boyfriends. Helping a daughter learn to drive takes advantage of many typically male strengths: directness, creating and following specific paths to a desired goal, and spending time in an oversized toy that goes *vroom*. We dads don't waste too much time thinking about how you might *feel* if you have to slam on the brakes or how it might affect the emotions of the driver behind you—just hit the doggone brakes, *now!*

Moms, on the other hand, often are stronger in skills and mind-sets valuable to becoming a classy driver: empathy, courtesy, and respect for others on the road. They're also far more willing to ask for directions when they're lost, which is a good reminder to our teens that we don't have all the answers and are not always in control. They're fully aware of how clueless we can be, but it's good for them to see that sometimes we simply don't know where we are and need the help of others.

7. Resolve conflicts with your teen's help.

Your advice or approach to a given driving situation may differ from the advice given to your teen by his driver education book or teacher. Your spouse may disagree with what you say, or your teen may simply not believe it's the best course of action. In some cases, there are multiple ways to execute a maneuver or handle a driving decision safely and skillfully.

When there's a conflict, talk about it with your teen, and get his opinion on it. Even if it's erroneous, his opinion needs to be heard and evaluated. Reach a compromise if you can, or hold firm if you believe strongly about something, but take his view seriously. Your teen may not agree with you in the end, but he will be more willing to consider it if he understands your reasoning and knows that you are at least open to considering another approach.

8. Do ongoing and postlesson joint evaluations.

Some suggest waiting until the end of a behind-the-wheel session to recap the ups and downs, allowing teens to focus on the driving. I prefer complimenting the good moves and pointing out errors as soon as they happen, then moving on (mostly because I don't trust my memory an hour later). Taking notes is a great way to record things as they happen, without disrupting your teen's concentration. Work it out with your teen according to her preference.

At the end of each session, do a general recap, and find out what your teen liked or didn't like. This doesn't need to be especially structured, but it can be a valuable way to keep on course. Ask open-ended questions:

"What was the most valuable thing you learned today?"

"Did anything that happened today really concern you or make you want to spend more time on it?"

"Anything I need to stop doing?"

Questions like these will allow you to summarize what you've observed and offer constructive criticism and positive encouragement. Solicit feedback on your style and whether you need to adjust it to keep from driving her crazy. Let her lead the debriefing on occasion, too. You'll get good insight into how she perceived the sessions.

9. You don't always have to be right.

Your role in helping your teen learn to be a better driver is not to be a driving instruction expert. It's to be a concerned, committed parent with more information than most. Both of you are in this together, and you'll both make mistakes. You'll scream at him when you vowed not to. He'll make that turn again and again without checking all his mirrors. Even with all your help and restrictions, your teen will still make bad decisions. Without them, however, he would certainly make even more. That's why you're doing this.

The point is to learn from the mistakes and keep working at it. Mistakes are often the most constructive learning opportunities. Your teen will appreciate your acknowledgment that you don't have all the answers and that you're not always right. You're just doing the best you can, and you're stuck with each other. Let him know that's the way you want it, too.

10. Your teen is forming lifelong habits.

Not to put any more pressure on you, but the driving habits, skills, and behavior you help instill in your teen during the first year or two of her driving will be carried with her for the rest of her life. She will probably drive somewhat less carefully when she's out from under your watchful eye, of course. But she is not likely to lose the fundamental concepts of visual scan, spatial awareness, braking, defensive driving, and crash avoidance. And especially if it's reinforced by your own behavior, her road manners—the demonstration of respect and courtesy for other drivers—will be evident in the years ahead.

11. You have incredible power . . . for a while.

Teens, like everyone, will work harder for something they really want. They really want the car keys. It's by far the most tangible (public) step toward adulthood they've taken in their young lives to date. The freedom, challenge, and responsibility represented by driving a car are very powerful motivators. As the keeper of the keys, you have an unusual amount of leverage and power over them. Don't waste it.

In the United States, depending on your state, your teen may be eligible for a license at 15 or 16, perhaps even with little or no required supervised driving. The laws that really matter here, though, are yours. There isn't a single state where a teen under 18 can obtain a driver's license without the written permission of a parent or guardian.

Whether it's the age at which you allow him to become official in the eyes of the state or the restrictions and conditions you give him as he learns to drive, you're in charge, and the consequences of inadequate maturity, experience, and preparation can be very painful.

12. Tell the story. Your teen will get the moral.

Remember when you were learning to drive? While you are helping your teen learn to drive, it's powerful to share your experiences. She needs to know you were scared, exhilarated, uncertain—that you made mistakes, had close calls, did stuff you never told your parents about. Teens view parents as pretty much ignorant of their world, so it helps to remind them that we've been in their shoes. Your stated goal should be to help your teen avoid many of the mistakes you made and become a much better driver at an earlier age than you were.

Resist the temptation to draw the obvious conclusions and morals of your stories, however. Your teen will get it. She won't tell you, of course, but she'll get it. When you say, "One time, I took a corner too fast, hit the gravel, got into a skid, and spun out. I thought I was going to have a heart attack," it doesn't need to be followed by, "So make sure you don't take corners too fast!" When you relate that it took you six months of allowance to pay back the scrape you inflicted on the side of your parents' Buick, she'll understand the message—it'll be her responsibility, too, if she scrapes your car.

Remember that in addition to imparting specific information, you are dealing in allegories, too. Tie together the parallels between how your teen behaves as a driver and how she behaves as a young adult. Remind her that how she treats the powerful machine you've entrusted to her is a clear indicator of how she'll treat future expensive possessions that demand respect, maintenance, and responsible use.

Finally, you may wonder what happens to all those well-chosen bits of information, snappy sayings, and repeated advice you will give to your teen. It's quite simple. They will be diligently stored in an expanding area of your teen's brain known as the *parentus lecturus*, which is Latin for "advice my parents repeat." It will reside there until she has her own kids, at which point parental hormones will trigger the release of these memories, and she will find herself saying to her kids exactly what you said. It's powerful, often infuriating, and unavoidable. So make your message matter.

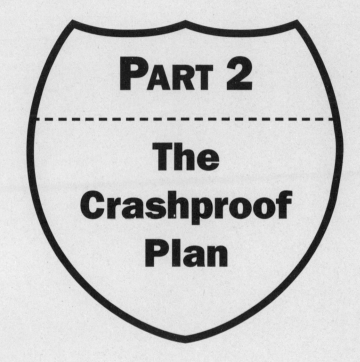

PART 2

The
Crashproof
Plan

First Gear: Safe, Smart Basics

Ideally, your teen's first on-the-road experiences will occur with a professional. Professional driving instructors are accustomed to anticipating situations that first-time drivers may experience, and they have the big advantage of another set of brakes in their training cars. You'll have to make do with stomping imaginary brakes on the passenger's side.

Whether your teen starts with a professional or not, however, your plan and the time you spend driving with him should be the same. No assumptions should be made about what he has "already done." Even if he's driven with a professional instructor and completed a driver education program, you have no idea exactly what driving exercises he's done and how skillfully he did each one. If your teen insists that he's already got that piece covered, tell him that this is a great opportunity for him to demonstrate that mastery to you.

Before you jump into the Crashproof Plan, remember that behavior takes time to hardwire. You could breeze through each of the driving sessions ahead in a fairly short period of time, spending perhaps 25 to 30 hours and a couple of weeks. Please don't.

The driving exercises and strategies are points of focus more than tasks to check off. They occur in a deliberate sequence so as to break down a complex task into specific steps. Your teen needs time to let each step sink in and build on the previous ones. Don't hesitate to repeat exercises, and don't be surprised if your teen regresses in some areas as he progresses in others.

During the Crashproof Plan, work in some unstructured driving time with your teen, too. Schedule time on the road where your intent isn't to complete a crashproofing session but rather to give your teen additional seat time and to give you a chance to observe his skills and behavior in a less goal-oriented manner.

Plan to involve yourself actively in your teen's driving skill development for at least a year *after* he gets his license, which is statistically the most dangerous year. Impart the message that he'll continue learning for the rest of his life, just as you are.

It's not hard to end up spending 80 to 100 hours behind the wheel over a 6-to-12-month period with your teen. And each one helps.

CHAPTER 5

Car Care 101

Time of session: 60 minutes

Locations: Your driveway, local service station

Never lend your car to anyone to whom
you have given birth.

ERMA BOMBECK

Have you examined the oil and fluid condition and levels in your car lately? Checked the tire pressure? Inspected your brake pads? With our busy schedules and the disappearance of full-service gas stations, routine upkeep and preventive maintenance on our cars often get neglected. Compounding this, today's cars are also monitored by an increasingly sophisticated array of computer chips and sensory devices. It's not surprising that many teens assume that routine maintenance is either unnecessary or someone else's responsibility.

Your teen should assume some responsibility for routine preventive maintenance and inspection, and it's easy to do. To begin, you don't even have to take the car out of the driveway.

1. Have her read the entire owner's manual of the car she will be driving, checking out everything under the hood, on the dash, and under the car as she reads. Go through it with her after she's finished, answering questions and quizzing her to make

sure she can point out and explain the most important parts and systems. It may seem like a pain to your teen, but the benefits are numerous.

First, she'll get a better sense of how a car actually works, a subject about which too many teens remain clueless. Learning the fundamentals of a car's operation makes it much easier to grasp important concepts—why oil and coolant levels are so critical to an engine's functioning, what a car's electrical system does, and how gasoline powers a car, for instance.

Second, she'll know where to check for oil, wiper fluid, coolant, and transmission, brake, and power steering fluid, and she'll be equipped to help with preventive maintenance.

Finally, she'll be able to locate things she probably hasn't even considered she might need: fuses, vehicle identification number, tool kit, and tire jack, among others, as well as all those odd gauges and buttons you seldom use.

2. While she's reading the manual, you create an "important information" worksheet. This will give your teen all the information she might need in the event of an emergency or a crash. Print up a sheet that looks something like the one here and contains essential information about her.

Name	
Address	
Home phone	
Work/cell phone	
Parent's work/cell phone	
Primary-care doctor, phone	
Neighbor, relative, phone	
Driver license number, state	
Car registration number	
Insurance company, policy number	
Auto club member number, phone	
Towing company phone	

IF YOU'RE IN A CRASH

- If you're OK, things will be fine. Cars can be replaced. You can't.
- Get yourself and the car off the road as far as you can.
- Put a flare on the road 50 yards or more behind your car.
- Dial 911 to alert the police, and then call home.
- Do not argue, blame, or admit error about the cause of the crash to others involved in it, or to anyone else. Just describe what happened, and only to the investigating police officer.
- Give the other driver and the investigating officer your license and insurance information.
- Get the names and phone numbers of any witnesses to the crash.
- Photograph your car, the other car, and the scene of the crash.
- Don't worry. We'll work this out.
- Write down the following information:

OTHER DRIVER(S) INVOLVED IN THE CRASH

Name	
Address	
Home phone	
Work/cell phone	
Driver license number, state	
License plate number, state	
Make, model, color of car	
Registration number	
Insurance company, policy number	
Insurance company phone	

INVESTIGATING POLICE OFFICER

Name	
Badge number	
Department	

Marti Stone, an attorney and a mother who has helped two teens learn to drive, reinforces the above, noting, "Make sure you keep a cheap camera in the car. If your child is ever in a crash, he should take pictures of his car, the other car, and anyone else involved. This is especially important if your teen is at fault, because you may get sued, and documenting everything is critical. Get the name, address, and phone number of everyone who witnessed the accident. Don't depend on the police to do it."

3. Review or replenish the key supplies and information carried in your car. Your trunk should contain:

> Quart of oil
> Windshield-washer fluid
> Blanket
> Bag of cat litter
>   for traction in ice and snow
> First-aid kit
> Can of pressured air for flat tires
> Jumper cables
> Emergency flares
> Two blocks of wood or bricks
>   (for chocking tires while changing a flat)
> Fire extinguisher
> Duct tape
>   (for sealing hose leaks)
> Spare tire, jack
> Tool kit
> Bottle of water
> Small shovel
> Rags
> Ice scraper/snow brush

Your glove box should include:

>Maps
>Small flashlight
>Pens, small notebook
>Extra sunglasses
>Wet wipes
>Tire pressure gauge
>Disposable camera
>Proof of insurance
>Owner's registration
>Owner's manual
>Important information worksheet

4. As specified in the car's owner manual, help your teen with the following:

Check the oil level, noting the condition of the oil, the date of the last change, and the manufacturer's recommended oil-change frequency. Emphasize the importance of maintaining both the oil level and the frequency of oil changes for maximum engine performance and longevity.

Check rubber belts and hoses for loose connections, leaks, and cracks, and inspect the engine and engine compartment for evidence of oil or other fluid leaks.

Check the fluid levels for windshield wipers, power brakes, power steering, transmission, and radiator. Make sure she knows the proper procedure for removing a radiator cap and adding antifreeze or coolant.

5. Head to your favorite gas station and have her perform the following tasks:

Fill the car with gasoline. It's a good lesson in the cost of operating an automobile to see those dollar signs whizzing by on the pump. *Caution:* Although cell-phone warnings are widespread, confirmed instances of sparks or static electricity from a cell phone causing a fire or explosion at a gas station are virtually nonexistent. That said, there may be some minimal risk, and there's absolutely no good reason to use a cell phone while handling a flammable liquid. A buildup of static electricity on people *has* caused many fires while fueling, however. This risk can be avoided in at least two ways. First, don't enter a car while refueling, because you could build up static. Second, get rid of static electricity before you handle a gas pump for the first or last time by touching a metal part of your car that is away from the gas-tank opening.

Clean the windshield, the windshield wipers, the outside rearview mirrors, and the headlight lenses. In a pinch, the acidity of a cola soft drink can help remove stubborn residue on windshield-wiper blades.

Fill up on any fluids that your earlier checks determined to be low.

Fill any tires needing air, as determined in the previous session.

Now, go do something fun together. You've just trained your teen to assume some important responsibility for upkeep of the car. Consider having her be responsible for the tasks in item 5 above whenever you stop for gas. She needs to keep in practice, after all.

CHAPTER 6

Connect with Your Tires

Time of session: 30 to 45 minutes
Locations: Your driveway, local service station

I had to stop driving my car for a while . . . the tires got dizzy.
STEPHEN WRIGHT

Within 18 months, three tires on our SUV went flat and couldn't be repaired, which was not only annoying and inconvenient but expensive. They were Michelins, a brand I have been faithful to and happy with for years. I was convinced that there was a defect in the tires, since each had experienced failure stemming from the sidewalls rather than punctures. I thought stories might soon appear in the national press about a faulty batch of Michelin tires, as with the Firestone debacle years earlier. Instead, it turned out to be my fault.

I had noticed that the tires had a tendency to be underinflated when I checked them, which was not often enough. It was also a heavy SUV, which our family of five fully loaded when we traveled. In short, I killed the tires by running them for too long on too little air with too much weight. And it took me until the third one to figure it out. Duh.

Tires are the Rodney Dangerfield of car components. They just don't get any respect. If there's one area of car maintenance that needs your increased priority and heightened awareness, it's your tires.

For this session, pull your car onto the driveway, and focus with your teen on one of the most important car-care aspects of being crash-proof: the tires.

The first exercise is to teach your teen how to change a flat tire. Practice on one of your good tires as follows:

1. Make sure the car is on a level surface.
2. Set the parking brake.
3. Block the tire diagonally opposite the flat one with two pieces of wood or bricks, one in front of and one behind this good tire. If one of the rear tires is flat, it's a good idea to block *both* front wheels.
4. Loosen the lug nuts on the flat tire.
5. Set up the jack as the owner's manual specifies, and raise the car until the (flat) tire clears the ground by several inches.
6. Remove the lug nuts, take off the flat tire, and mount the spare (remount the good one he's practicing with).
7. Tighten the lug nuts, but not fully.
8. Lower the car, and remove the jack.
9. Tighten the lug nuts as firmly as he can with the lug wrench, and remove the tire blocks.

Next, teach him the importance of maintaining proper tire pressure. You'll need a good air-pressure gauge. It's impossible to tell whether a tire is underinflated by looking at it, unless it's practically flat. Never trust the pressure gauges on the hoses at gas-station filling units. They're notoriously inaccurate, adding potential injury to the insult of having to pay for the stuff that surrounds us in unimaginable quantities.

1. Have him check the air pressure of each tire. The tires should be cold, which means at least three hours after driving or before they have been driven a mile. If you have to drive more

than a mile for air, first determine how many pounds of pressure each cold tire needs. Then check the inflation again before you fill the tire, and add the original pressure deficit to the warm inflated pressure.

For example, let's say your tire's proper inflation is 40 pounds per square inch (psi) of pressure. Your cold reading is 32 psi, which is 8 pounds low. You drive several miles to the station, and the same tire now measures 34 psi, because it has heated up on the way there. You still need to add 8 pounds to get the correct cold inflation of 40 psi.

According to a government study, more than a quarter of all cars and trucks on the road in the United States have at least one substantially underinflated tire, defined as 8 or more psi below the recommended pressure. Underinflation is a serious safety hazard. The rollover crashes of Ford Explorer SUVs in the 1990s were attributed partly to tires that overheated and failed because of low pressure. Tires with insufficient air pressure also impair handling, hurt fuel economy, and wear unevenly. Insufficient tire pressure is serious enough that federal regulators have mandated that all new passenger cars and trucks must have individual tire-pressure-monitoring sensors by the 2008 model year. Microchip sensors will trigger a dashboard light if a tire falls 25 percent below the recommend inflation pressure.

2. Teach him about contact patches. Take a look at the size of the page you're reading right now. Each of your tires is connected to the road at any given time solely by a patch of rubber not much bigger than that, and those little contact patches are responsible for a car's traction. Maintaining control of a vehicle is all about traction, without which you can't steer, accelerate, or decelerate. Antilock braking, four-wheel drive, and

stability and traction control systems can all help maximize a car's braking and handling, but none of them actually provides more traction. That's the job of your tires.

Tire manufacturers are so prominent in all types of professional auto racing because tires often spell the difference between winning and losing. On the most sophisticated Formula 1 car, the engine, transmission, suspension, and internal computers all are in service to the fraction of a tire that actually makes contact with the track at any time.

It's the same with your car on the road. The only thing connecting all 6,000 pounds of your average behemoth SUV to the road are those four small patches of rubber. They slow you down, keep you on the road, and move you where you want to go. You need proper tire inflation to keep those contact patches working most effectively. Just as with professional racers, it makes a huge difference if your tires have good tread and are properly inflated.

3. Teach him how tire air pressure naturally varies. Myths and conflicting information abound about tire pressure and correct inflation, but the most important facts are the following.

Tire pressure naturally varies with outside temperature, going up or down at least 1 psi for every 10-degree-Fahrenheit increase or decrease in temperature.

Tire pressure naturally builds up, usually by several psi, just from the heat generated by driving.

Tires normally lose air over time, at least 1 pound of pressure per month in cold weather, even more in warmer weather. It's not unusual for tires to lose 10 pounds of pressure over a period of several months, more than enough to cause overloading, excessive tire wear, and increased risk of premature failure.

Metal valve caps will help maintain tire pressure better than plastic ones.

The solution to maintaining proper tire pressure in all conditions and seasons is simple: follow the original equipment manufacturer's guidelines. Always keep your tire pressure at the level recommended on the sticker found on your car's door, fuel lid, or glove box.

4. Let him know that tires get tired, too. Rubber compounds in tires get brittle and degrade with age, and even unused tires can fail simply because they are too old. Most tire experts warn against using tires older than six years. A tire's manufacture date can usually be found embossed near the inner edge of the sidewall, as part of the tire identification number or serial number. The last four numbers indicate the week and year the tire was made. For example, if the last four numbers are 1701, it means that the tire was made during the 17th week (May 9 through May 14) of the year 2001.

5. Show him how to examine tires for tread wear and depth. Maintaining adequate tread is essential for a tire's grip and performance. Examining the tread depth also gives him a chance to notice any irregular wear, a sign that other areas such as alignment and suspension may also need attention. Tires should have at least an eighth of an inch of tread remaining, and they're legally worn out when they have only one-sixteenth of an inch of tread depth left. A reasonably accurate way to check whether your tires have enough tread is to put a penny (Lincoln's head first) into one of your tire's grooves. If the top of Lincoln's head remains visible, the tire needs replacing. Remember this trick with the following saying: "If you can see Lincoln's head, you don't have enough tread."

6. Consider snow tires. If you live in a region with winter weather, you'll optimize tire performance and safety by using snow tires. All-weather radials do an adequate job in all conditions, but snow tires are far superior in cold, snowy, and icy conditions and will go a long way toward helping keep your teen crashproof. The rubber compounds that make up today's snow tires don't get brittle in cold weather, which increases the stickiness and grip in cold as well as low-traction conditions. Using snow tires will extend the life of your warmer-weather tires and increase safety in conditions where it's needed the most.

7. Drive to the nearest service station, and have your teen add air pressure as needed to each tire. I can almost guarantee he'll be adding some air.

Give your tires some respect, and teach your teen to change a flat, maintain proper air pressure, and check for tread wear. Rotate your tires regularly, at least every 10,000 miles, and keep them aligned and in balance. Check the inflation pressure weekly, just before long trips, and whenever the car will carry extra loads.

Even better, have your teen do it. It's a great way for him to pitch in and help pay you back for all the hours you're spending with him, grinding your teeth and losing your hair.

CHAPTER 7

Start Your Engines

Time of session: 45 minutes

Location: Large, empty parking lot

*You can take either the hare or the tortoise approach to
crashproofing your teen. Remember who won that race.*

THE AUTHOR

Are you both ready to go? It's time to get the motor running and
the car on the road. Drive your teen to the biggest, emptiest parking lot you can find, which is the safest place for her to demonstrate or
learn the basics of piloting a two-ton piece of machinery.

Start with the pre-drive checklist, a ritual that should be followed by
your teen every time she gets behind the wheel.

Do a walk-around.

Have your teen walk completely around the car and make a quick
inspection of the inside and outside of the car before she gets into
it. When the car is parked on the street, make sure she always faces
traffic as she walks counterclockwise around the car. This may seem
a tad compulsive, but there are at least half a dozen good reasons to
develop this habit, which include determining if any of the following exist:

- A flat tire.
- Bumper or paint damage or dents.
- Anyone inside the car who shouldn't be.
- Evidence of oil, coolant, or transmission fluid leaks.
- Adequate space, front and back, to allow getting out of a parallel-parking spot.
- Anyone or anything behind the car. This is especially important when backing out of garages and driveways, since young children are often hard to see from inside a car. Every year in the United States, several dozen children are accidentally killed by family members who back up and run over them.

Establish a comfort zone.

Adjust the driver's seat, with your teen's shoulders against it, so that he's a good foot away from the wheel if your car has an air bag, and so that his wrist joints rest on top of the wheel at 12 o'clock. A more upright seat creates better posture and attentiveness. Set the head restraint so that the top is level with the top of the driver's head, not at neck level where it's often set. Adjust the steering wheel to a position where he can see over it and it's comfortable.

Check the dashboard.

If she's not already familiar with them, review all the dials, knobs, levers, buttons, and gauges on the dashboard and within reach of the driver. Have her tell you in her words the function of each. These tend to get short shrift by parents and even driving instructors.

- *Headlights.* Headlights should always be on. Keeping headlights on during the day can measurably reduce crash rates by making her car easier to see for approaching vehicles. Several studies of daytime running lights show an average reduction in crash rates of about 7 percent, and a Danish study reported a 37 percent decline in left-turn crashes in the first 15 months after implementing required daytime running lights. You won't significantly reduce the life of your headlight bulbs or battery or add meaningful load on your generator or alternator. One turn of a knob may gain your teen a measurable advantage.

- *Oil and temperature gauges.* If your car has gauges instead of idiot lights, review with your teen what constitutes danger levels. You'll be less likely to have expensive engine problems caused by low oil or inadequate coolant if she gets into the habit of periodically checking them.

- *Parking brakes.* Have her apply the parking brake and try to drive down the driveway a bit, so she knows exactly what it feels like when the brake is on and when it's off. Many teen drivers have damaged parking brakes because they were not aware that they were on, thinking that the car was simply very sluggish. She should also understand that it's good practice to put this brake on whenever the car is parked on an incline.

- *Ignition switch.* Most cars do *not* need the accelerator pressed when the car is started. Many newer cars are very quiet after ignition, and it's not uncommon for new drivers to forget the car is running and turn the key again. That awful grating sound will discourage her from doing that again.

- *Emergency flashers/hazard warning lights.* If your teen runs out of gas, is involved in a crash, or ends up stopped on the side of the road in trouble, she'll need to know how to turn the emergency flashers on and off. The car should always be pulled off onto the shoulder of the right lane.

- *Cruise control.* Young, inexperienced drivers should not use cruise control at all, but it's especially dangerous in the rain or on slippery roads, where it can cause the car to hydroplane. Reinforce this with a quick rhyme: "Cruise in the rain, bruise on the brain."

- *Air bag light.* Be aware of the "check air bag" light, especially if you have a car built before 1990. If it stays lit or blinks, flashes, beeps, or chimes for more than seven or eight seconds after starting the car, have it checked out immediately by a service technician to avoid malfunctions or premature air-bag deployment.

Secure the seat belt.

We've heard ad nauseam about the importance of wearing seat belts, and it's had an effect on adults, where usage rates are quite high. Teens, however, wear them far less than older drivers, and it's still the single biggest factor in surviving a crash. Nearly two-thirds of teens killed in crashes weren't wearing seat belts.

That's instructive. It means that, unlike most adults, many teens haven't internalized the benefits of seat-belt use. That's your job, because although seat belts and air bags don't have much to do with making your teen crashproof, they have everything to do with helping your teen *survive* a crash. Review these facts with your teen.

- Seat-belt use cuts a front-seat car occupant's chance of dying in an accident by half and by as much as 80 percent in an SUV rollover.
- Being belted in gives him a much better chance of retaining control and consciousness in a crash, since it's difficult to maintain either while he's smashing through the windshield or bouncing off the roof.
- Being ejected from a car in a crash increases the chance of injury or death by 300 percent.

• Seat-belt use combined with air bags results in far fewer deaths and injuries than just seat belts; air bags used alone can actually cause serious injuries.

People are far less aware, however, of how important it is to their teens' safety (let alone their passengers') that their backseat passengers also wear their belts. While most states have seat-belt laws, fewer than a third of them require backseat riders to buckle up. You should, though, to prevent your teen from becoming a human crash-test dummy.

Unbelted backseat passengers, like any unrestrained object in the car, become high-velocity projectiles in a crash. If the person behind your teen isn't fastened in, your teen is nearly *four times* as likely to die, because of the impact of his passenger's body rocketing into him in a frontal crash. Make it a nonnegotiable rule: anybody in the backseat has his or her seat belt fastened. To reinforce this, ask your teen to imagine his backseat friends hurtling toward him at 90 feet per second as he politely insists that they buckle up . . . parent's rules, you know.

Adjust the seat belt and shoulder harness to fit your teen snugly. Most vehicle shoulder harnesses can be adjusted to a lower setting on the door pillar to fit them better.

Get a grip.

If you imagine the wheel as a clock face, her left hand should grip at 10 o'clock and her right hand at 2 o'clock. The thumbs should be up, pushing against the front of the wheel in a golf-style grip, rather than wrapped around the wheel in a baseball-style grip. In this position, the thumbs are less likely to be injured or dislocated by the deployment of an air bag. It also offers a much surer grip on the wheel. Demonstrate this by handling her a smooth, round pen and asking her to grip it in a fist, with the thumb curled around the fingers. Then pull the pen up and out of her hand. Now have her grip it with the thumb up and pushed against the barrel of the pen. It's nearly impossible to take it out of her hand.

Many schools still teach hand-over-hand steering, but it can be cumbersome and is even illegal in some countries. A much better turning style is the pull-push method. When turning right, for example, the right hand pulls the wheel down until the right hand reaches about the 5 o'clock position. At the same time the left hand should slide down to the 7 o'clock position. The left hand then takes over the grip and the right hand relaxes, while the left hand pushes the wheel up to the 12 o'clock position and the right hand slides up to meet it at that position. Repeat the process until the turn is complete, then reverse it as the wheel returns to its straight-ahead position. The arms never cross or go beyond the 12 o'clock position, and the wheel should never slip through the hands. This method of turning keeps the hands in closer range to their normal position and allows for a 180-degree turn without lifting them off the wheel. In a collision, it will also keep the arms away from the top of the wheel and out of the area where the air bag will deploy, at about *200 mph*. Facial bones have been shattered by the force of an air bag exploding and forcing a driver's hands back into the face.

An additional bonus to this method of handling the steering wheel is that with both hands always on the wheel at the 10-and-2 position, it's impossible for a teen to make a phone call, apply makeup, or grope a favorite passenger.

Mind the mirrors.

Adjust both exterior side-view mirrors so that in his normal seated driving position, your teen can see a sliver of his vehicle in each mirror. After the mirrors are adjusted, stand outside the car several feet away from the driver's-side mirror. Step straight backward slowly while your teen observes you in the side mirror until you can't be seen. Continue moving back until you are back in sight, and repeat it several times on each side of the car until your teen knows where the blind spots begin and end on each side of the car.

To practice dealing with those blind spots, have him pretend (while sitting in the car) that he is about to pass a car, change lanes, or simply drive in reverse. The proper sequence is:

1. Check the rearview mirror.
2. Check each exterior mirror.
3. Glance back over each shoulder to make sure there is no object or car within either side's blind spot.
4. If all is clear, engage the turn signal and begin the maneuver.

Repeat several times to build repetitive memory for this crucial process, which is ignored by many drivers. This sequence is the *only* way to ensure maximum safety while passing, changing lanes, or backing up. In addition, whenever he is in the blind spots of other vehicles, his risk increases, so he should know to spend as little time there as possible. If he finds himself in a possible blind spot of a car in a lane next to him, for example, he should speed up or slow down to get out of that zone.

Here's another tip involving mirrors. If your car has a vanity mirror on the passenger sun visor, adjust it so it becomes your own rearview mirror while your teen drives.

Fix the feet.

Foot positioning gets scant attention with beginning drivers, but it's vital. First, only the right foot is used for both the gas pedal and the brake, never the left. Ever. Second, shoes must be worn. Barefoot is out. Third, when moving the right foot from the gas pedal to the brake pedal and back again, the heel does not lift off the floor. The foot pivots on the heel, which stays planted while the upper foot swivels back and forth between the pedals. This may seem like a small point, but the natural tendency of new drivers is to lift the foot completely off the gas, slide it over, and press on the brake. This takes an extra second, which at 45 mph means that your teen will travel an extra *66 feet* before *beginning* to brake, which can be the critical difference in avoiding a crash. So make sure that her heel is a fixed pivot point, placed between the gas and brake pedals.

Now that the pre-drive check is finished, it's time for your teen to get behind the wheel and do some exercises.

Practice parking perfectly.

Begin by having your teen repeatedly pull into and out of different parking spaces in the lot. Challenge him to see how close he can come to parking the car exactly between the lines. Most new drivers will initially pull too close to the line on the driver's side. Have him get out each time to note the car's placement.

Next, have him see how closely he can line up the end of the front bumper with the end line of the parking space. Both exercises help develop your teen's spatial awareness of the vehicle, crucial for avoiding scrapes and fender benders, especially when he starts parking the car in your garage. A more extensive session on developing parking skills can be found in Chapters 8 and 9.

Practice these parking exercises until he has made major improvement, or until he begs to stop, whichever comes first.

Accent the accelerator.

Have him drive in a straight line across the lot without using the accelerator, to understand how the car moves without additional help from the gas pedal. Then cross the lot again with the gas pedal slightly depressed, going maybe 10 mph, so he can gauge the relationship between pedal pressure and acceleration. Continue at slightly increasing speeds across the lot, up to 20 or 25 mph or to the limit of safe speed in the lot.

The goal for now is to develop a good feel for the degree of accelerator pressure needed for the slow speeds driven in parking lots. Have him continue varying the accelerator pressure while slowly driving around the lot until he's slowing down and speeding up smoothly.

Begin with the brakes.

Next, have him practice going forward and backing up using only the brake pedal. Increase the speed and brake pressure a bit until he is comfortable with stopping more quickly. Focus on brake-pedal pressure by having him brake carefully and smoothly as he drives slowly around the lot. Similar to the accelerator practice, the point is to build muscle memory in the feet so that stopping and starting are smooth and well modulated. More comprehensive braking-skill exercises are covered in Chapter 10.

Tame the turns.

As simple as it may seem, learning to turn accurately is extremely important at this stage. Because we've been doing it so long, it's easy for us to forget all the discrete steps we unconsciously take when we do something as simple as making a turn. It's not instinctive for your teen, however. For example, a teen sees a left-hand turn coming up and may think about activating the turn signal, braking, and turning the wheel.

In reality, it's a bit more complex and should happen more like this:

1. Well ahead of the turn, check the rearview mirror for the following distance of traffic behind you.

2. Check both side mirrors and blind spots for any side traffic or obstacles.
3. Engage the turn signal.
4. Ensure that you're positioned correctly and in the proper lane.
5. Begin braking for warning and to begin slowing down.
6. Check the rearview and side mirrors again.
7. Check traffic entering the intersection from right and left.
8. Gauge the status of turn signals and other stopped cars' positions.
9. Continue braking smoothly, checking all mirrors.
10. Come to a full stop at the sign or intersection.
11. Before turning, check oncoming and left and right traffic patterns once more.
12. Complete the turn.

Even a simple left-hand turn requires a 12-step program! If your teen slides on any of the steps, the odds increase that eventually he'll be unpleasantly surprised, because problems typically are caused by others, often in unexpected ways.

Beginning drivers often crash because the arc of their turn was flawed or because they entered a turn too fast. Practice slow, broad turns at first, seeking accuracy in circling light poles or parking-space markers. Then have your teen turn in figure-eight patterns, to practice smoothly linking turns in opposite directions.

Next, move to turning tighter circles at slightly increasing speeds, so he can feel the difference in steering response. Some teens will initially prefer turning in one direction over the other, so have him make lots of left and right turns to make sure he's equally comfortable and competent in both directions.

When you're both comfortable with these initial exercises, have him leave the parking lot and drive around a quiet neighborhood, practicing smooth acceleration, braking, and turns. Work on developing turning accuracy until he can consistently achieve a smooth arc into the middle of the lane he's turning into. Many beginning drivers tend to make left-hand turns too early, cutting off some of the lane they're turning into, and right-hand turns too late, straying too far from the curb or right lane. Make your teen aware of these general tendencies, and help him initiate left turns a little later and right turns a little earlier than he might instinctively do.

Crash data indicate that many beginning drivers lose control simply by entering turns at too high a speed, overcoming their tires' traction. Reinforce that braking and any necessary reduction in speed needs to occur *before* initiating a turn. Help your teen remember the importance of slowing down well before a turn with this rhyme: "To avoid getting burned, coast the most in a turn."

Practice the steps outlined in this chapter until you feel your teen is ready to move on to the next challenge: going backward.

Going Backward

Time of session: 30 to 45 minutes
Locations: Empty parking lot, local neighborhood

*I had to take more than 50 hours of training to get certified
to carry my handgun. I've never pulled it out.
I drive a car eight hours a day, sometimes at high speed
in pursuit, and I've never had any training with that
4,000-pound weapon.*

Police officer, Adrian, Michigan

My friend Ben Slocum relates this story: "The son of a friend of mine, who shall remain nameless, had an exhilarating experience when he was about sixteen. He was with his mother and was backing down their rather steep driveway. When he got near the end of the driveway, his mother told him to hit the brakes, but he hit the gas instead. He shot across the street, over the curb, roared across the neighbor's lawn, and blasted through a picture window, coming to rest in the living room of their neighbor's home. Unfortunately, a couch was in front of the picture window, and the neighbor's grandmother was sitting in it. Grandma flew about 15 feet across the living room. Amazingly, she escaped without a scratch. That's one way to enter a home, I guess."

That does give new definition to *breaking and entering*.

Driving in reverse often gets little attention in driver training, but doing it skillfully will help your teen avoid fender benders (and grand entrances like the one above).

1. Head back to that big, empty parking lot, because now it's time to go backward.

2. Have your teen grip the wheel at the 12 o'clock position with his left hand. He should look over his right shoulder, and his right arm should be draped over his seat. Watch the natural tendency for his left hand at the top of the steering wheel to turn to the right as his head turns to look over his right shoulder. If this happens, be sure to point it out. He must focus on keeping his left-hand movement separate from the movement of his right shoulder and his head.

3. Many beginning drivers accelerate too quickly when backing up, so have him back straight out of the driveway slowly, with his foot *off* the gas, using only the brake to control speed. Whenever possible, your teen should use only the brake to control speed when going backward. In some cases, that won't be practical, because he'll need to get out into traffic quickly. But consider this: *if the foot is always covering the brake while backing up, your teen should never hit the accelerator by mistake.*

4. Let him get a feel for the effect of steering-wheel adjustments on the back and front ends of the car. Your teen will not automatically turn the wheel the correct way to make the car do what he wants it to do in reverse. Just tell him to *steer in the direction he wants the back end to go.* If he wants the rear of the car to go toward the right, simply turn the wheel to the right, and vice versa. Practice driving in reverse in the parking lot

while he's looking over his right shoulder and making slight turns and corrections back and forth.

5. Next, have him practice driving in reverse using the interior rearview mirror and both exterior side mirrors, becoming aware of the advantages and disadvantages of each mirror. The rearview mirror gives a broad view immediately behind the driver but is restrictive on the sides and is sometimes obstructed by head restraints, passengers, and poor rear-window design. The side-view mirrors are essential for avoiding fender benders in tight spaces and maintaining awareness of cars beside and behind the car, but each has blind spots.

6. Finish by having him practice backing into and out of parking spaces until he can position the car in the middle of the space every time, without adjustments.

PARALLEL PARKING

Now he's ready for parallel parking. This is often postponed until later in a driver's development, but it's good to do it very early, because it requires many of the skills that will help keep him crashproof at higher speeds: spatial awareness, mirror and visual checks, fine steering-wheel adjustments, and good modulation of the brake and accelerator pedals.

Have your teen follow these steps:

1. Pull into a parking space, and drive forward into the space ahead of it.

2. Check the left mirror (to guarantee that in a street situation, no cars are directly behind him).

3. With his foot on the brake, back up slowly into the space to the right and behind him, as if the parking space immediately

to his right were occupied by a car. Crank the wheel hard until the left rear corner of the car is even with the (imagined) left front corner of the car he is parking in front of.

4. Turn the wheel in the opposite direction, and slide into the parking space, looking over his right shoulder and using the right side mirror for guidance.

You should be outside the car in the (empty) parking lot helping him decide when and how hard to turn the wheel in each direction. When he miscalculates and it's clear he will not be able to pull into the space without hitting the imaginary cars in front or in back of him, have him start over again and correct his mistakes.

Practicing with empty parking-lot spaces gives him a risk-free way to learn how to drive in reverse into tight spaces. He should practice doing this from both sides, because on one-way streets, he may need to back in to the left. Don't worry about him being able to do this perfectly now.

When he has become proficient at parking in the imaginary spaces, take the next steps:

1. Drive to a nearby neighborhood where you can find several consecutive empty parking spaces, giving him a large area to maneuver into, and practice parking there until he does it well several times.

2. Find a different parking spot, where there is only one empty space and cars bracket both ends.

3. Have him approach that space and line the car up beside the car *behind* the open spot he wants to pull into, put his turn signal on, and stop. This tells the cars behind him that he's going to park and also eliminates the possibility of traffic be-

hind him occupying the space he needs to back into the spot, which can happen if he starts by pulling next to the car *ahead* of the open space.

4. Have him move up alongside the car in front of the parking space, about two feet away and lined up steering wheel to steering wheel. Have him begin backing up straight until his body gets even with the back wheel of the car beside him. Then give the steering wheel one full turn, and back into the space, while looking in the left rearview mirror until he can see the front *right* headlight of the car behind him.

5. Unwind the wheel to the left, and he should end up parallel in the space.

6. If necessary, you can get out of the car and onto the sidewalk, and help guide him into the spot.

7. Make sure he's aware of front-end swing. He probably won't initially realize how far the front of his car can swing out while parallel parking. If he is backing up into a space on his right, at maximum wheel crank on a narrow street, his left front end could extend over the center lane divider. As he practices backing into the space, make sure he is aware of where the car's left front corner extends. Clearance is needed from cars in the oncoming lane, and cars behind him may pull out around him as he is parking.

8. Continue practicing until he can get into and out of the space without multiple attempts or bumper touches.

REVERSING ON STREETS

Next, practice going backward by having your teen back into and out of driveways on neighborhood streets.

1. Begin by having him turn right into a driveway and back out of it. Make sure he looks left, right, then left again before he enters the road and that he guides his way backward by looking over his shoulders. Have him finish backing out to the right, then continue in the same direction he was originally going and do the same exercise at the next driveway.

2. When he can do that smoothly and consistently, pick out another driveway, and have him turn in to the right and back out to the left across traffic and into the opposite lane. Keep in mind that many teens initially back straight up out of the driveway and across traffic, so coach him to *give the wheel a good turn as soon as his front end clears the driveway.* In most nonpractice cases, there will be traffic coming both ways when he does this, and there is little time to correct the steering. Practice until he can back out into the opposite lane and head in the opposite direction with precision.

3. Have him practice the best way to reverse direction: turning left across traffic into a driveway and reversing out to the right. When many beginning teen drivers want to change direction on a street, they will choose to turn right into a driveway and back out across traffic into the other lane. But it's easier and safer to turn left, even across traffic, into a driveway across the street and back out to the right, because then you don't cross traffic in reverse.

4. Finally, practice aborted reversals. Begin with either a right turn into a driveway or a left turn across traffic, but the next

step is the same. Tell your teen to back out of the driveway until the rear end of his car just enters the street, then pretend that he's changed his mind (there's an oncoming car he didn't clearly see, for instance), and shift quickly to forward gear and go back up the driveway. This exercise reinforces the sequence of brake-shift-gas needed to get quickly back off the road, and helps hardwire this as preferable to hurrying to complete a dangerous maneuver.

Backing up may seem like a small, routine procedure, but it can get you into trouble, as Ben Slocum's story proved. I'll give you another one, more personal.

After attending a commercial driver education program and getting her permit, my daughter Brittany spent seven months driving with me and my wife and accumulated more than 80 hours behind the wheel with us. Brittany's a responsible young woman and had developed solid fundamental driving skills, too. She looked forward to getting her license and wasn't happy when I reminded her that we still had a long way to go and that we'd continue working with her for at least the next six months or so, as needed. She was pretty convinced she was ready to drive on her own and had a hard time understanding why her training would need to continue.

She was nervous on the day she was to take her driving test and get her license. By the time she got behind the wheel with the person administering the test, her palms were sweating. She was asked to pull into a residential driveway and back out onto the street, reversing direction. Brittany looked both ways, put the car into reverse, and began to back out of the driveway. As she entered the street, a school bus appeared from "out of nowhere", bearing down on her. Startled, she hit the accelerator instead of the brake and shot farther out into the road, then quickly braked, shifted, and pulled back into the driveway, completely shaken. She didn't get her license.

We had neglected to practice the "what if" situation of step 4 above: What if you had checked both ways before backing out of a driveway onto a street, thought it was clear, but as soon as you started to enter the street, you saw a bus (or a bike or a motorcycle) coming right at you? Well, it seems simple enough. You brake quickly, shift from reverse to forward, and give it some gas to get your tail end out of the road, right? She hadn't done that before, though, and her subconscious hadn't been trained to do that sequence of events instinctively.

On the way home, despite having been warned about reduced traction as a result of a light snowfall, she approached a traffic light at the same speed she normally did on dry roads and felt the tires skid momentarily. In less than half an hour, these were the lessons learned:

- It's one thing to drive competently and calmly in a familiar situation. With an authority figure, a new location, and a license on the line, mistakes can be made.
- Your vision can fool you. It's impossible for a 40-foot-long, 9-foot-high bright yellow school bus to burst from out of nowhere. She looked, her brain told her it was clear, and she went. She *looked,* but she didn't *see.* There's a big difference.
- We'd talked about speed and the effect of snow and water on traction. Now she felt it firsthand. She'll remember next time.
- Maybe she wasn't quite ready to be completely on her own after all.

That night, she practiced backing out of a driveway, braking, and moving back into it, simulating the earlier situation. She made sure she didn't just glance both ways, *expecting* it to be clear. She *looked* both ways, and let her brain take a second or two to really *see.*

The next day she went back, passed the driving test, and got her license.

Brittany's embarrassing incident also gave my wife, Sherri, and me an opportunity to 'fess up to her. I failed my first driving test, too. Couldn't parallel park well enough. Her mother failed hers, too. Rolled through a stop sign. So we told her it was hereditary, and she could lay some of the blame on her genes. That made her feel a lot better, knowing that she was following a family tradition.

We all make mistakes. If we're lucky, we learn from them and don't repeat them. But when driving, it takes only a second for a mistake to become very costly.

That's why you're doing this.

CHAPTER 9

Protect Your Bubble

Time of session: 30 to 45 minutes
Locations: Your garage, local neighborhood, shopping mall

The safest teen driver is one who knows his parents are watching.
RICARDO MARTINEZ, FORMER HEAD OF NHTSA

Driving a car safely can be compared to maneuvering a bubble within a bubble. Our car is a protective bubble of steel and glass, and we keep it crashproof by maintaining a safe bubble of space around it at all times and in all conditions. In this session, you'll focus on improving your teen's spatial awareness of her vehicle and its surroundings.

To help give her a more innate sense of her vehicle's dimensions, begin this session at home, having her practice pulling into and out of the garage. This not only helps develop spatial awareness, but it's also good preventive maintenance for your garage. Countless teens have inadvertently remodeled their parent's garage while learning to drive.

1. Have her practice backing straight out of the garage and pulling straight back in. Her initial tendency will probably be to leave too much space on her side and not enough on the passenger side. Stand well out of her way at the back of the garage as she practices, pointing out where she should stop.

Find an object or landmark in the garage to help her line up the front end of the car, or hang a tennis ball from the ceiling to mark where the car's front bumper should stop.

2. If your garage requires a turn in from your driveway, have her experiment with different turn entry points to find the best arc to get to the middle of the door opening. Stay out of the car to guide her the first several times.

3. If possible, practice with different cars to improve her spatial awareness. A teen will often emerge from the garage and tell her parents, "I was used to the Corolla," after she has just scraped up your bigger vehicle.

During the first several weeks of learning to drive, Brittany scraped our SUV on the side of our garage door and was very worried about my reaction. I shrugged it off, told her the scrapes were no problem and that they might even come out with some rubbing compound. (That would be some miracle rubbing compound.) She was relieved and got the valuable message that it was only paint and metal, not really important at all.

I then went into the basement to a place where screams could not be heard and mourned the first scratches the car had ever received, after more than six years and 130,000 miles.

4. When she's shown competence managing the vehicle's dimensions in the garage, head to a quiet residential neighborhood, where traffic is light and your teen can practice driving on two-way streets. Neighborhoods are good places to work on spatial awareness, since she'll need to assess and adjust her car's position relative to parked cars on her right and oncoming cars on her left.

5. As she becomes more adept at positioning and maneuvering the car on residential streets, work on improving her use of mirrors. Mirrors are your teen's second set of eyes, letting her know what's going on around her while minimizing the time her eyes are off the road. Conflicting opinions exist about how often a driver should check her mirrors, but many experts recommend about every eight seconds. While that may seem excessive, with practice it becomes a virtually unconscious habit. In the meantime, remind her to check her mirrors frequently with brief but focused glances.

Any time your teen plans to turn, the mirrors need to be consulted before signaling and again just before initiating the turn. Likewise, whenever your teen needs to brake, the rearview mirror must first be checked (except in an emergency stop). If a driver behind her is tailgating and not paying attention, a mirror check before braking can give her some options to avoid a rear-ender—abort the turn, change lanes, or find an escape path, for example.

6. Focus on the passenger-side mirror. On many newer cars, this mirror can present a troublesome illusion. Because the mirror is convex to afford a wider range of view, it causes objects to appear to be farther away than they really are, hence the printed warnings that "objects are closer than they seem." Your teen needs to account for this distortion when she determines the spacing of cars behind and adjacent to her. The best way to do this is to have her check the passenger-side mirror for a following car, note the image, then look over her right shoulder to see how far back the car really is. She can then compare that with any visual information from her rearview mirror to adjust for the true following distance of a car behind her.

7. Quiz her periodically as she drives to reinforce good mirror use. Ask her if there is anyone driving behind her. She should be able to tell you without looking in her mirrors. Do this a few times, and you'll see more frequent mirror use, if for no other reason than to be ready the next time you ask. Tell your teen that it would be very impressive if she could accurately describe the driver and the vehicle behind her using at least four adjectives. Reinforce the importance of using the mirrors frequently with the following rhyme: "To avoid the coffin, use the mirrors more often."

8. Teach her to assess the various zones surrounding her car. Have her imagine an extensive bubble of space—a very expensive and fragile bubble—that extends out around each side of the car and protects her and the car. Her forward vision helps guard the front bubble, and the mirrors help define and protect the back and side areas of the bubble. Anything that pokes into the space and pops the bubble—curbs, cars, pedestrians, bikes, garage walls—is a potential disaster.

Dr. Frederick Mottola, a consulting author of the *Drive Right* series of driver education books and creator of the Zone Control System, developed a space-management model that relies on managing and protecting six zones surrounding a vehicle: left front, front, right front, left rear, rear, and right rear. He defines each of these zones as the width of a lane, extending as far as the eye can see. Each zone is considered to be either open or closed as a sight line, a travel path, or an escape route at any given time.

An open zone means you have a clear line of sight toward your path of travel into that zone and can move into it without restriction. A closed zone has a sight restriction or an obstructed path of travel. An escape path is an open zone where your car can go to avoid an impending obstruction or collision.

Your teen should continually assess which zones are opening and closing, an especially important habit for when she quickly has to evaluate a potential escape path. When a change of speed or direction is needed to prepare for changing conditions ahead or to avoid an immediate threat, options can be quickly chosen based on which zones, or sections of the bubble, afford a view, travel path, or an escape route.

Integrate her mirror use and zone control with this exercise:

1. Identify each zone for her. Front is the area immediately in front of the car. Left front and right front can be observed by turning the head and scanning peripherally in either direction. The rear zone requires a view from the rearview mirror, and side mirrors or over-the-shoulder looks give views of the left rear and right rear zones.

2. Call out each zone surrounding the car, identifying it as either open or closed as a view, a travel path, or an escape route. For example, if you're traveling on a two-way residential street:

    "Front zone is open for a view and a path (unobstructed ahead). Front right is closed (parked cars). Front left is open for a view or escape route (no cars in the other lane). Right rear is closed (parked cars), rear is closed (car following closely behind), left rear has an open view (no car passing on the left)."

    By going through this exercise, the driver can determine that, for example, if a child suddenly darts from between the parked cars on her right, she can instinctively steer into the left lane to avoid him, because she's already determined that it's open for both a view and an escape route. If she develops an ongoing read of which zones afford vision, travel path, or escape, she can react much more quickly to changing circumstances.

On a divided highway, your commentary might be more like this:

"Front zone is closed (obstructed by truck). Rear is open (no car following behind). Left front and left rear open for view, travel path, and escape route (open lane). Right front and right rear are closed (cars ahead and behind in the right lane)."

In this instance, if the truck in front of her were to slam on the brakes, she could choose to brake hard if there were enough time (since no cars are behind her), or she could move immediately into the left lane, since it's open as a travel path.

3. Now have her do the same, calling out each of her zones and identifying whether they are open or closed for a view, travel path, or escape route.

4. Help develop her awareness of activity surrounding and beyond the road's boundaries. For the first several times driving in neighborhoods, you need to be especially vigilant about the more immediate potential problems—car doors opening, kids on bikes, hard-to-see signs, pedestrian crossings—as your teen concentrates on navigating the streets and protecting her bubble. As she gets more confident, use crashproof commentary and verbally point out additional things she should be aware of—pets in yards, people in parked cars (who may suddenly open their doors), and traffic indicators several blocks ahead.

You're teaching her the beginning phases of scanning, a mental and visual discipline of consciously and unconsciously monitoring multiple environmental factors simultaneously. That's a long-winded way of saying she should maintain a constant state of mental and visual alertness unlike anything she's probably ever done. It's that important, and it's covered more fully in Chapter 11, "Developing Raptor Vision."

Encourage your teen to be conscious of the space her car occupies and protective of the areas surrounding it, by continuously monitoring her bubble and the zones surrounding her car. Reinforce the concept with this rhyme: "To stay out of trouble, protect your bubble."

AVOIDING BUBBLE TROUBLE AT THE MALL

Does your teen appreciate a good excuse to go to the mall? Well, now you've got one, because this part of the session will take place at her favorite shopping center. Mall or shopping-center parking lots introduce heavy low-speed vehicle and pedestrian traffic and are excellent places to practice space-management, parking, and scanning skills. Because of all the action, busy parking lots are also the scenes of many fender benders and near misses. An unpublished study by the Insurance Institute for Highway Safety found that about 14 percent of auto damage claims in a metropolitan area involved parking-lot collisions.

The more comfortable your teen is in this situation, the less likely you'll be visiting your body shop with a check in hand. Here's how to practice getting in and out of busy parking lots with your car and your sanity intact:

1. Have your teen cruise up and down the parking lanes in the lot, signaling as she turns down each lane. She may feel like a bit of a dork, but other drivers will appreciate the advance notice. Make sure she drives in the center of the lane, in order to be equidistant from cars pulling out on either side, unless there is a car coming down the opposite way.

2. Make sure she covers the brake pedal the second she sees a backup light. People backing out have the most obstructed

vision, and this also positions her to move into the space. Instruct her to use her turn signal while she is stopped and waiting for the car to back out.

3. Using *only the brake pedal* to control speed, she should pull forward into the parking space, stop, then back out again. Point out the difficulty she has in seeing behind her as she backs out, and remind her that if she parks between tall vehicles—trucks, SUVs, vans—her vision will be even further reduced.

4. Again using only the brake pedal to control speed, have her practice *backing into* that parking space, stopping, and then pulling out. Point out how much better the visual information is with this method, and let her know that backing into and pulling forward out of a parking space is the preferred way to park. She'll see better, brake more quickly if need be, and be less likely to be hit by other cars.

5. Continue with her driving around the lot, and practice parking, especially backing into a space. As she drives, use crashproof commentary to identify the critical little things—doors opening, backup lights coming on, people stepping into her lane, drivers failing to stop at stop signs, and shopping carts rolling across the lot. Stress that she has to be especially wary of pedestrians. Most adults seem to consider every inch of a parking lot to be their personal right-of-way, and young children don't know any better.

Additional tips for surviving large, congested parking lots:

• Enter the lot from the side rather than the main entrance, for lighter traffic.

- Point out to your teen all the scratches, dings, and dents on the doors of the cars parked in the mall. Most people in parking lots open their doors with little regard for the doors of other cars parked beside them. Remind your teen always to open her door carefully and avoid parking too close to other cars.
- Park on the far outskirts of the lot. In addition to having more available parking spaces, you'll get far fewer door dings and dents, and you both can probably use the walk. Exercise relieves stress.
- Keep your headlights on for greater visibility, even in the daytime.

I actually enjoyed going to the mall to practice space-management and parking skills with my daughter. Those mall trips were among the few where I didn't end up with a major credit card bill a month later.

CHAPTER 10

Stop It! Braking Skills for Life

Time of session: 45 minutes
Locations: Empty parking lot, rural road

If you ever run into what's in the way,
most likely you failed to miss it.

BOB GREEN, RACING INSTRUCTOR, FOUNDER OF
SURVIVE THE DRIVE

One of the early challenges I discovered in working with my daughter was in accelerating her braking-response time. She would see traffic slowing down ahead and know that she needed to brake, but by the time she decided to put on the brakes, we would be closing too fast on the car ahead, and I would be saying, "Brake. Brake harder. Brake!"

After several sessions of practice, she began to develop a better feel for closure rates and appropriate braking pressure and speed, and I no longer had to raise my voice, at least about braking.

Before we begin the braking exercises in this chapter, some information about braking systems and braking techniques is in order.

The first thing you need to do is understand the braking system on your car. Do you have an antilock braking system (ABS)? If you have ABS, is it four-wheel or two-wheel?

NON-ANTILOCK BRAKES (DISC OR DRUM)

Before the development of antilock brakes, maximum braking effectiveness was achieved by skilled cadence braking, or pumping the brakes. Some older vehicles on the road today do not have antilock brakes, and cadence braking must still be used. Cadence-braking technique involves pressing the brakes until just before the tires lock up, backing off *slightly*, then deploying pressure again until near lockup, backing off slightly, and so on, until the car reaches the desired speed. The trick is to exert maximum brake pressure without locking up the brakes and losing steering control.

ANTILOCK BRAKES

Most newer cars have ABS. Antilock brakes are a major advance in braking technology, consisting of wheel-mounted speed sensors combined with electrohydraulic braking circuits. Rotating wheels provide more stopping force than skidding wheels, and steering control is lost when tires lock up and skid. ABS monitors wheel speed and keeps them rotating by very rapidly (up to 18 times per second) changing the pressure in the car's brake lines to maintain maximum braking, just short of locking up the wheels. In other words, this is automated cadence braking.

When you press hard on antilock brakes, your feet may feel a distinctive pulsing or vibration, the pedal could suddenly drop, or there might be a clicking or grinding noise. New drivers often think this means there's a problem and back off the brake, but it simply means the system is working. Braking properly with ABS means keeping your foot firmly pressed on the brake, without pumping, and letting the system work.

Antilock braking is primarily designed to help a driver maintain control and be able to steer around a hazard while emergency braking.

Antilock brakes are not designed to stop the car more quickly, although they often will if used correctly, especially in wet or slippery conditions. If you are skilled at cadence braking, ABS brakes will not always stop you in a shorter distance than non-ABS brakes. In some cases, in fact, such as loose gravel or heavy snow forming a wedge in front of the tires, ABS may actually lengthen stopping distances. ABS will often end up getting you stopped more quickly and safely if used correctly, however—with constant, hard pressure.

Most passenger cars equipped with antilock brakes have four-wheel ABS. Light trucks, vans, and SUVs may have either four-wheel or two-wheel ABS. Vehicles with two-wheel ABS, which affects only the *rear* wheels, may still lock up the front wheels during emergency braking, with some loss of steering control. Make sure you and your teen are familiar with the braking system of your vehicle, and practice proper techniques in varying conditions until you're accustomed to the sound, feel, and braking results.

Surprisingly, a number of studies indicate that antilock brakes have not made significant, if any, reductions in the number of car crashes. A major reason for this is that many people just don't use them properly. Virtually all of today's parents learned to drive cars without antilock brakes, and many still use the same technique with their cars today, which do have antilock brakes, negating their built-in advantages. A survey of drivers with ABS revealed that more than 50 percent of motorists in North Carolina and 40 percent in Wisconsin thought they should pump the brakes. Don't make the same mistake.

BRAKING PRINCIPLES AND TECHNIQUES

The next essential element in acquiring advanced braking skills is to understand some basic principles of braking, as well as the safest and most effective braking techniques.

Contrary to what you might assume, the most successful road racers are those who master the brake, not the accelerator. Any yahoo with a functioning right foot can crank a car up to top speed on a straightaway. The masters of the pedal to the left are the ones who win. Those who brake most skillfully make it around the track in the least time.

Those who master the brakes also stay the safest. You'll never run into anything if you're not running. And if you must run into something, you're better off running into something as slowly as possible.

Braking occurs in three phases. First, your brain has to think about stopping and recognize that a braking action is required. That takes most drivers an average of 1.75 seconds. The next phase, getting the foot from the gas pedal to the brake pedal, typically takes another 0.75 seconds. At 65 mph, during those 2.5 seconds, your car will travel 80 percent of the length of a football field. Combine that with the beginning driver's tendency not to brake firmly enough, and you can see why this is such an important basic skill to develop.

Eddie Wren, the founder and executive director of Drive and Stay Alive and one of the most highly trained driving instructors in the United States, offers the following illustration of braking phases in more detail:

	40 MPH	50 MPH	60 MPH	70 MPH
REACTION/ THINKING/ DISTANCE	40 feet	50 feet	60 feet	70 feet
BRAKING DISTANCE	80 feet	125 feet	180 feet	245 feet
OVERALL STOPPING DISTANCE	120 feet	175 feet	240 feet	315 feet

But here's the kicker. These figures are absolute best-case scenarios. They assume dry pavement and a braking reaction time of just 0.67 second, which requires a very alert driver. The National Safety Council publishes similar information with an assumption of more than 2.0 seconds for reaction time, which would nearly double these overall stopping distances. Wet or slippery roads can more than double the distance yet again. So the key variables to braking are the driver's reaction time, braking technique, and road conditions.

When beginning drivers encounter uncertainty in a driving situation, their first response is often to get off the gas and coast while they watch things unfold or decide what to do next. This response needs to add a critical step. A key tenet of crashproofing is this: your teen's automatic reaction to uncertainty or rapidly changing conditions should be to *get his foot off the gas pedal and immediately rest it on the brake pedal.* "Covering the brake" in this manner saves valuable time if he does end up needing to brake and is the safest response while he is evaluating actions that don't require an emergency response. As Gordon Booth, president of Advanced Drivers of America, notes, "At 40 mph, covering the brake puts 40 feet in the 'braking bank,' since you've saved the time needed to move the foot from the gas pedal to the brake pedal."

Emergency stops require different responses, and emergency braking can often be the difference between a crash and a close call. In the course of helping your teen become crashproof, you may need to tell him to come to an emergency stop, because he didn't see a child run into the street or a car running a red light, for example. Here's what you *don't* want your teen to do in this instance:

- Try to figure out why you made the request.
- Get off the gas until he decides whether to brake or not.
- Get off the gas and cover the brake.

You want him instead to *get on the brake right now,* and his braking technique needs to be instinctive.

Head back one more time to that big, empty parking lot, because you're both going to work on stopping—not slowing down or coming to a smooth stop, but emergency braking.

This exercise may be a bit hair-raising at first for both of you, but it's essential, and it's very seldom taught in driver education programs. Most beginning drivers are hesitant to brake hard enough, mistakenly thinking that they'll hurt the brakes, hit the windshield, or lose control. Your teen needs to know exactly how a vehicle responds and how much brake pressure it takes to stop *right now* at lower speeds. And you're going to show him first, by "driving in his shoes."

First, determine whether your car has antilock brakes or not and, if so, whether the ABS is four-wheel or two-wheel. Do the following exercises yourself first to demonstrate to your teen and remove a bit of the apprehension. Then have your teen do the same exercises in the same sequence.

FOR ANTILOCK BRAKES

Start at the far end of the parking lot, and have your teen get up to about 15 mph, then brake hard. Make sure that he does not pump the brakes but instead keeps a steady, firm pressure on the brakes until stopped. Practice this a few times until he gets a feel for the brake pressure needed to come to a complete stop at this speed.

Do the same exercise at gradually increasing speeds—20 mph, 25 mph, and finally 30 mph—until he can consistently and smoothly bring the car to an emergency stop, feeling how the car reacts at each speed. This exercise will hone your teen's reaction time from gas to brake and reinforce proper foot positioning. Remember, his right foot should not lift off the floor to shift from the accelerator to the brake. It should instead pivot on the heel.

When he can demonstrate improved brake control and stop quickly (if not smoothly) at each successive speed, add the element of steering while braking, developing his stomp-and-steer skills. In many emergency braking situations, the best course is to brake hard and steer straight ahead if possible, because braking hard and veering in any direction can be a dangerous combination. But sometimes an obstacle needs to be avoided, and your teen will have to steer while braking. *Stomp and steer* is one of the more important skills crucial for crashproofing teens whose cars have antilock braking systems. Here's how to develop the stomp-and-steer technique:

1. Place an object, such as a cone or a cardboard box that can be clearly seen (and you don't mind if it gets run over), in the middle of the parking lot. Have your teen approach the object closely at 15 mph and brake hard when he's about 20 to 30 feet from it.

2. He should come to a complete stop before hitting the object, if possible. If he can't, he should attempt to steer around it *while maintaining firm brake pressure.* (If his car has rear-wheel-only ABS, he may need to back off the brake pedal slightly if the front wheels begin to lock.) His eyes should be fixed not on the object as he steers around it but on the path he wants to take to avoid it.

3. Increase the speed in 5-mph increments until 25 or 30 mph. Work on stopping quickly and smoothly, while he gains the confidence to continue braking while steering around the object. He'll quickly realize that the higher the speed, the more difficult stopping before the object becomes, and he'll also learn how to steer around an object successfully while braking—stomp and steer.

To reiterate, with ABS:

- Brake firmly, and keep the foot on the pedal.
- Do not pump the brakes.
- Maintain or increase brake pressure, look where you want to go, and steer carefully to avoid trouble if necessary.
- With rear-wheel-only ABS, follow the above, but back off the pedal slightly if the front wheels begin to lock.

The ability to use his car's braking system reflexively for maximum effectiveness will get your teen out of many dicey situations on the road.

FOR NON-ANTILOCK BRAKES

If your car does *not* have antilock brakes, your teen will need to spend a little rubber before he can know how much to modulate brake pressure to avoid locking up the wheels.

1. Start at the far end of the parking lot, and have him get up to about 15 mph, then brake hard. Practice this a few times until he gets a feel for the brake pressure needed to come to a complete stop at this speed.

2. Do the same exercise at gradually increasing speeds—20 mph, 25 mph, and finally 30 mph—until he can consistently and smoothly bring the car to an emergency stop, feeling how the car reacts at increasing speed. At each speed, have him brake until the point of tire lockup, then back off and resume brake-pedal pressure until the car is completely stopped. The point is for him to stop as quickly as possible in as short a distance as possible without locking up the tires. It will take

many repetitions for him to begin to feel how hard to pump, how much to back off, how quickly to resume pressure, and so on, but this skill is essential for crashproofing if your car does not have antilock brakes.

3. When he can demonstrate improved brake control and stop quickly at each speed, add the element of steering while braking. Place an object, such as a cone or a cardboard box that can be clearly seen, in the middle of the parking lot. Have him approach the object closely at 15 mph and brake hard when he's about 20 to 30 feet from it.

4. He should come to a complete stop if possible before hitting the object. If he can't, he should steer around it. Emphasize that if he locks up the wheels, he loses steering control, but if he modulates the brake pressure to avoid lockup, he can steer around an object while maintaining brake pressure. His eyes should be fixed not on the object as he steers around it but on the path he wants to take to avoid it.

5. Increase the speed in 5-mph increments until reaching 25 or 30 mph. He'll quickly realize that the higher the speed, the more difficult stopping before the object becomes. Have him work on hard braking without locking up the tires and steering carefully around the object.

When you feel your teen has become proficient with the above exercises in a parking lot, find a stretch of road with no obstacles or traffic in either direction, and take the next step in braking-skill development.

As your teen drives, let him know that when you say "Stop!" and slap a hand against the dashboard, he should come to a stop as quickly and safely as possible. This should not be a tire-burning panic stop but a firm, controlled brake and, for safety's sake, should be done at speeds no greater than 40 to 45 mph. This exercise helps ensure that if and when you need him to make an emergency stop, his focus will be on the braking and not on the reason for your request. (It's also a compulsory testing technique in many countries.)

You may, however, find yourself in a situation where he's about to collide with something and is not taking appropriate braking or steering action. Be prepared in an emergency to assume control of the wheel and help steer out of trouble. Tell your teen that if you need to help him in an emergency, you may end up having to grab the steering wheel, and he should not panic or fight it.

Braking skills, such as automatically covering the brake when conditions change and knowing how to brake in an emergency, are especially important for your teen's next driving location. Neighborhoods provide plenty of instances where your teen will need to stop quickly because of kids, balls, pets, and cars entering the road from all directions.

Shifting into Second Gear

To teenagers, having done an exercise right once qualifies them in their minds to move on to the next step, and they will want to move ahead quickly. Resist this temptation. The point is not for your teen to have demonstrated that he can do a driving exercise perfectly one time. It's to do it perfectly many times—when he is tired, stressed, or bored; when the weather is not ideal; when traffic is heavy or unpredictable; when other drivers are annoying or dangerous. The goal is to have him react appropriately and instinctively to each driving situation simply because he has done it so many times before.

And that takes repetition. It will probably be time to move on to Second Gear only after he has been begging you to do so for the past three or four driving excursions. Use the following checklist as a guide to help you and your teen know when he is ready to move to Second Gear.

First Gear Accomplishment Checklist

_____ Knows basic car controls and adjustments.

_____ Can do a complete pre-drive check.

_____ Hands and feet are positioned correctly.

_____ Is aware of blind-spot locations.

_____ Can successfully park accurately in non-parallel spaces.

_____ Has mastered beginning skills for parallel parking.

_____ Has had initial practice with accelerating and braking.

_____ Has had initial practice turning left and right.

_____ Can back cleanly and accurately into a parking space.

_____ Is familiar with stomp-and-steer braking technique.

_____ Knows the braking system of the vehicle.

_____ Driver adjustments and pre-drive check are habitual.

_____ Turns wheel correctly when maneuvering in reverse.

_____ Is proficient in backing in and out of driveways.

_____ Has mastered intermediate skills for parallel parking.

_____ Uses all mirrors frequently and consistently.

_____ Brakes and accelerates smoothly and consistently.

_____ Has good awareness of car's spatial positioning.

_____ Turns precisely and smoothly in both directions at intersections.

_____ Exhibits growing awareness of all surroundings and environment.

_____ Is beginning to parallel park consistently and accurately.

_____ Fully understands all traffic signs and right-of-way rules.

_____ Shows sound decision making in new traffic situations.

_____ Is familiar with beginning scanning techniques.

Second Gear: Getting Comfortable

Your teen is now more comfortable operating a car in low-stress driving environments such as parking lots and residential streets. It's time to increase the challenge and complexity of his or her driving experience, building skills and confidence in commonly encountered driving situations. It's time to shift into Second Gear.

Second Gear driving sessions emphasize the importance of developing excellent visual search and awareness skills and how to use them in driving situations with increased risk, such as intersections.

Navigational skills involving reading maps and not getting lost are also stressed, along with the principles of vehicle balance and following distances.

In Second Gear, the continued development of a defensive-driver mentality is encouraged by incorporating "what if?" scenarios into the driving sessions, where your teen can mentally rehearse appropriate actions.

In addition, the development of better concentration and awareness is encouraged. Television, movies, computers, and video games have all accelerated the trend toward shorter attention spans, and most teens aren't accustomed to the type of consistent mental focus demanded when driving a car. The longer behind-the-wheel sessions will help improve your teen's ability to sustain focus while driving.

Developing Raptor Vision

Time of sessions: 30 to 60 minutes

Locations: Country road, less traveled streets

Don't worry that children never listen to you;
worry that they are always watching you.

ROBERT FULGHUM

Have you ever watched a hawk search for prey while perched on a tree limb or in flight? Raptors (eagles and hawks) have some of the sharpest eyes in the animal kingdom, simultaneously monitoring the smallest movements half a mile away as well as those very near them. Their eyes constantly move, scanning a vast area. Their survival depends on it.

Likewise, your teen's continued survival in an automobile depends in large part on her visual search (scanning) skills. Failure to see other vehicles is cited by some as the number one cause of crashes involving teen drivers. To avoid crashes, drivers must simultaneously monitor highway structures and surfaces, traffic signs and signals, other vehicle actions, and nonvehicle traffic such as pedestrians and bicycles. It can be overwhelming at first, but it's absolutely essential.

Your challenge in this driving exercise is to help your teen develop her own raptor vision, a systematic scan for potential hazards and for information she will use to help crashproof herself. Developing good visual search skills in your teen involves getting her to expand her area of focus and to process greater amounts of visual information more rapidly. New drivers tend to focus narrowly on the immediate road ahead of them, in a kind of tunnel vision. But it's often what's outside that limited frame of reference that needs the most attention.

Fortunately, with practice, the brain gets more efficient at filtering and categorizing what it's processing. Reds and yellows will subconsciously register as warnings. Peripheral movement will attract her eyes and trigger a response more quickly. Closure rates will be calculated and accounted for more automatically.

1. Before you begin, make sure your teen wears a high-quality pair of sunglasses designed for driving, polarized for glare reduction, and with good UV protection. Make them fashionable, so she'll wear them, but avoid tiny or dark lenses. Driving glasses should be used in most daytime driving conditions, not just on those blinding sunny days. They'll reduce glare, her eyes will tire less quickly, and she'll gain protection from harmful UV rays, helping to keep that raptor vision sharp.

2. Find a country road or quieter street with relatively long stretches of uninterrupted pavement. Your first task in developing your teen's raptor vision is to increase significantly the distance down the road where her eyes search. Ask her to identify the farthest point down the road where her eyes focus, to determine how far ahead she typically looks. Then help her find a spot twice that distance ahead, and have her practice maintaining the outer edge of her visual field at that distance.

   The goal is gradually to increase her focal distance to where she looks down the road with a 15-to-25-second lead time. At highway speed, that means roughly one-quarter to one-half mile ahead. This shouldn't be a fixed reference point but rather the far end of a constantly shifting visual scan that begins a minimum of 600 feet (two football fields) ahead of her car and ends at least a quarter-mile up the road.

At 60 mph, it takes at least 200 feet to stop, and that's with dry pavement and rapid braking reaction time. A focal distance of 600 feet still leaves only a few seconds of lead time between deciding to brake and ending up stopped.

Your teen may initially be concerned that with a lengthened forward scan, she'll be less attuned to what's immediately in front of her, but she'll find that her mind can process much more information far more quickly than she realizes. With practice, her ability to monitor the road immediately ahead will not suffer by increased focus on the road farther ahead. In fact, focusing farther ahead simply gives her more time to react to what soon ends up immediately in front of her. Help extend your teen's habitual forward scanning distance by pointing out signs, cars, intersections, and landmarks much farther ahead than she's accustomed to monitoring.

3. In addition to increasing her straight-ahead focal distance, your teen also needs to increase the *width* of her visual scan, so augment her increased forward scan with an expanded peripheral scan. Most peripheral scans of beginning drivers end at the boundaries of the road lanes. Expanding this scan enables drivers to see and assess additional potential threats such as cars approaching intersections or pedestrians nearing crosswalks. Have her point out homes, buildings, and landscape features well off the side of the road and give you a verbal running account of what catches her eye in the surrounding areas.

4. Next, work on getting her in the habit of constant eye movement. Too many drivers employ a fixed stare, with most of their time spent looking straight ahead. Like a hungry raptor, she should keep her head and neck moving, with her eyes always looking for movement and assessing the next decisions. Instruct her to practice continually moving her eyes from near to far, from forward view to peripheral view, from rearview mirror to side mirrors.

Work on a forward scanning system that continually alternates between a 15-to-25-second outer boundary and an ongoing road scan at about half that distance, and a rear scanning habit that uses rearview and both side mirrors.

5. As she becomes proficient, work on a more systematic way to alternate between visual ranges. Her scans should focus in and out among three visual ranges:

Immediate action range

The immediate action range encompasses a scan of about 2 to 5 seconds ahead. In this area, drivers must execute without thinking, and it's where emergency braking skills are critical. The immediate action range is where crashes are *reactively* avoided.

Scan and plan range

The scan and plan range is covered by a scan of from 6 to 12 seconds ahead. This is early-warning territory, where "what if" scenarios are best employed and good scanning skills can *proactively* avoid a crash.

Crashproof range

In this range, the scan is beyond 12 seconds, covering traffic and conditions up to a mile ahead. The crashproof range is where your teen can observe the reactions of traffic ahead and get early notice of where it's slowed down or backed up. Here, your teen can choose appropriate action with the luxury of several different alternatives, as things ahead develop.

Let's say that your teen notes brake lights way up the road. She now has time to check her mirrors and see which zones surrounding her car yield open or closed pathways. She can then tap her brakes to warn following drivers, while deciding whether to slow down or take other action to prepare for the probable traffic backup ahead. The crashproof range is also where teens become smoother, more consistent drivers, making smaller, more frequent adjustments of speed and position farther ahead of time.

Ideally, these raptor vision exercises will help your teen develop a scanning system that becomes unconscious, and she will regularly monitor her surroundings without even thinking about it as she drives.

CHAPTER 12

Intersections

Time of session: 60 minutes

Location: Residential or rural intersections

*A careful driver is one who honks his horn
when he goes through a red light.*

HENRY MORGAN

One of the most dangerous stretches of road my teens need to navigate is only two blocks from our home, the first intersection they encounter after leaving our driveway. Cars from our subdivision enter without a stoplight onto a very busy stretch of two-way highway. The average speed of traffic is 50 to 60 mph, and from one direction the cars come around a fairly sharp curve. Finding an adequate gap in traffic to pull out onto this road is difficult and leads to several close calls every week.

Teens do not have a well-developed sense of the time in which a car will reach a certain point at a given speed (the closure rate). My daughter initially tried to calculate enough room to squeeze in front of oncoming traffic, but she wasn't accounting for the safety and annoyance factor of making the oncoming cars slow down. It became clearer to her when a driver tailgated her to make a point after she pulled out in front of him.

To ensure your teen's safe entry onto roads, help him develop a better awareness of closure rates and how they can affect his safety at intersections and merges.

1. Park a short distance away from a busy highway intersection, and find a safe place near the road to observe the passing cars. Have your teen pick out cars in the distance and estimate how many seconds he thinks it will take for them to reach your spot. Have him count off the seconds—"one one thousand, two one thousand, three one thousand," and so on—and see how close he can get to the actual time. He'll soon have his eyes better trained to gauge the time it takes for the average car to close the gap.

   Note to your teen that closure rate is a function of both speed and distance. Figuring out how long it takes for the typical car to go a certain distance is the first step. But a car going way over the speed limit will cross that distance much more quickly. Your teen must observe a car for a *few seconds*, rather than taking a quick glance, in order to gauge that particular car's rate of speed. Then he can know whether he has time to pull out or not.

2. At a busy intersection your teen frequently encounters, select distinct landmarks that can act as trigger points to help determine whether he should enter traffic. At the intersection I mentioned earlier, my daughter and I chose marker points in both directions to help her identify when it was safe to pull onto the highway. From the west, it was a sign about a quarter-mile down the road. If an oncoming car had already passed that sign, it wasn't safe to pull out into that lane. From the east, we identified a tree at the beginning of the curve. In order to pull out across traffic, cars had to be behind the landmarks in both directions.

3. Drive to several lightly traveled urban or residential streets, to build in additional complexity and distractions and give him practice with stoplights and intersections. Intersections are especially fertile areas for collisions, fender benders, and near misses, accounting for nearly 40 percent of all crashes. Your teen's scan meter has to be set on high for every intersection, because there is so much going on that he needs to monitor. The key is to start assessing the intersection long before he gets there. Use crashproof commentary to reinforce verbally what his mind needs to be processing, and do it a hundred yards or more ahead.

For example: "OK, that light up ahead has been green for a while, so it's stale. It may go to yellow before you get through it, so ease off the gas. Check your mirrors for traffic behind you. See that truck at the light in the opposite lane? He's going to want to turn left in front of you, and he's going to do it before the light turns, so watch him."

Reduce the risk of intersection turns by having your teen check the mirrors and signal well ahead of his turn and tap his brakes to alert drivers behind him. When he is in a left-hand-turn lane waiting for traffic or a light, have him keep his front wheels straight rather than pointed toward the direction of the turn. If his car is rear-ended with its wheels turned, it could get pushed into oncoming traffic.

Your teen should have the mind-set that tells him a turn signal means that somebody *might* turn at some point. It also might mean that driver has had the signal on for the past five miles and is blissfully unaware of it. To be safe, don't let your teen pull out in front of a car with a turn signal on until he sees the tires beginning to turn.

4. Reinforce red-light caution. Most beginning drivers assume that other drivers will always stop at a red light. They don't. Every year, more than 900 people die and almost 200,000 are injured in crashes that result from red-light runners. In a Virginia study conducted at five busy intersections over several months, a motorist ran a red light an average of *every 20 minutes*. The most frequently reported urban crashes result from drivers running red lights, stop signs, and yield signs.

Remind your teen how frequently red lights and other traffic signs are violated. When going through an intersection after stopping at a red light, help him remember the likelihood of red-light runners with this phrase: "Red-runner rule: Assume there's a fool."

Always assume that someone will run the red light, and have him hesitate before moving for a good two to three seconds after the light turns green. That's long enough to buy him enough time to avoid most red-light runners but not delay the drivers behind him too long. In New York City, of course, this maneuver will immediately result in a chorus of honking horns. (Driving in New York City, however, is best done in an armored tank with additional strategies beyond the scope of this book.)

5. Establish clarity about yellow lights. Yellow lights mean "caution," but that's pretty ambiguous. Most adult drivers interpret yellow lights to mean "hurry through before it turns red." Don't teach your teen that tactic. The timing settings that turn lights from yellow to red vary enormously (often from three to six seconds), as does the traffic congestion at a given intersection.

Teen drivers should consider a yellow light to mean "stop

at the intersection" (unless they have already entered it when the light changes). The fact is, many red-light runners aren't brazen enough to blow through a fully red light. Often, they approach the intersection at the tail end of a yellow light, and by the time they reach the intersection, the light has turned red. The net result is the same, though. They've made an illegal maneuver, and people moving quickly off a green light into the intersection can collide with them.

Many teens will worry about drivers behind them, and they do need to be aware if they have a raving tailgater on their bumper before stopping as a yellow light is about to turn red. They should already be aware of such a creature prior to approaching the intersection, and it's more important to decrease their odds of an intersection crash than to worry about annoying or causing a tailgater to have to brake.

6. Teach your teen to stop a full car length behind the line at a light if he is first in line. This will give cars and especially trucks more room to complete a turn in front of him and adds a small cushion of time as he pulls into the intersection after the light changes. If he is not first in line, he should stop behind the car in front of him so that he can see both its rear wheels plus an additional three feet. This gives enough room to maneuver if his car is hit, if the car in front of him breaks down, or if he needs to escape from a potential carjacking or similar threat.

7. Before entering any intersection, make sure your teen always looks left-right-left, then right again before moving or turning. His head and neck as well as his eyes need to move, and it should be an unconscious habit at every intersection: look left-right-left-right, then proceed.

8. Practice turns with an awareness of teen tendencies. As mentioned earlier, new drivers often initiate left-hand turns too early, cutting off some of the lane they're turning into, and initiate right-hand turns too late, cutting it close to the curb or right lane. Point this out to your teen, and keep an eye on these tendencies as he makes turns.

   Females have a statistically greater crash involvement at intersections, so pay particular attention to this area with girls, especially turning left across traffic. Practice left turns across traffic repeatedly, making sure she observes the two-to-three-second hesitation at lights and stop signs that buys her an extra margin of safety before entering intersections. Teach her to scan several cars ahead in the lineup coming toward her, so she can spot cars, motorcycles, or bicycles which may be hidden behind larger vehicles.

9. In approaching any intersection controlled by a traffic light, there is a *stop/go decision point,* the spot beyond which a driver is committed to continue through the intersection, because there isn't time or space to stop the car safely. This point should be about two seconds before entering the intersection. If your teen reaches the stop/go point as the light changes and must choose whether to continue through or stop, he needs to make a rearview-mirror check. If a heavy truck is on his tail, that may be the deciding factor for continuing through the intersection to avoid a rear-end collision. Stress that he should already know how close someone is behind him before he gets to the stop/go decision point.

   If he is not being tailgated and passes the stop/go point as the light changes, he shouldn't speed up or slow down. Instead, he should continue at speed with a quick scan of all sides before going through the intersection, in case someone heads into it just as he passes through.

If your teen finds himself on a collision path with a car, it will be hard to predict accurately whether speeding up or emergency braking would be better to avoid a crash. When in doubt, he should brake. Slower speeds are always preferable to faster ones in a collision, and his braking may give the oncoming car enough room to get through the intersection in front of him.

You can help your teen determine stop/go points by identifying where you think each one is at different intersections. Then have him point out where he thinks the stop/go point is at the next several intersections.

It also helps to scan ahead to pedestrian walk/don't walk signals. They give early warning of a light about to change and alert your teen to the possibility of pedestrians rushing across before the light changes.

10. Make sure he understands and practices proper right-of-way at various kinds of intersections. At roundabouts, rotary intersections, and traffic circles, drivers must yield to traffic coming from the *left*. At three-way, four-way, and all-way stops, the first one to come to a full stop goes first. What's less well understood is that if two drivers arrive at about the same time, the driver on the *right* has the *right*-of-way.

When it comes to respecting rights-of-way, when in doubt, *give your right away.*

CHAPTER
13

Making the Familiar New

Time of session: 30 to 45 minutes
Locations: Local neighborhoods, town

I cannot teach anybody anything,
I can only make them think.

SOCRATES

Do you believe that your teen is most at risk for a crash on high-speed freeways or in unfamiliar cities? Actually, she's at highest risk near home in her most familiar surroundings, at average speeds of 45 mph or less. Why? First, that's where most of her driving will occur, so simply with extra exposure the odds of a crash are greater. Second, it's precisely because it's familiar territory that her scan alertness is more easily dropped down a notch or two. She's been in a car on those stretches of road dozens and dozens of times. Yet she's never really had a reason to take note of what makes a particular route unique or to analyze it for hazards. The areas near your home, school, and town will be so familiar to her that she might not even know the names of most of the streets. And it's that slackening of awareness that will come back to bite her. She may feel that she can be on cruise control a bit, and she may back off on the scanning skills and raptor vision.

Your objective during this session is to help your teen see with new eyes on her most familiar routes.

1. Start by "driving in her shoes" on the two or three most frequent routes your teen will take in her next several months of driving: to school, to work, or to her best friend's or grandmother's house, for example.

2. As you drive, break the routes down into segments, pointing out areas where she needs to be especially aware. This takes the general "Be aware" and moves it to the specific "Be aware of this particular spot every time you approach it for this reason." The more specific the better. Your teen has a harder time remembering and putting into action the reminder "Look farther ahead down the road" than she does "As soon as you come over this rise, always check Burr Road, half a mile down on the right, because you can see whether anyone is stopped and might pull out in front of you." By making it all seem a little new and different, you'll subconsciously trigger the same mental alerts in the future as she drives those routes.

   The goal is gradually to help her build a new mental map of her most frequent driving locations and tune up her scanning and awareness in those areas. You're also creating a framework for use in unfamiliar situations, because the needs are similar: how far she can see, where the obstructed views are, what might happen based on traffic patterns ahead.

3. Find the most hazardous stretches of these routes—the busiest intersections, the obstructed-view corner, the point where the bike trail crosses—and identify driving problems and solutions for each. These are the places where your teen is likely to have the most ongoing risk, and there are usually pre-

dictable occurrences at each of these heavily traveled spots.
For example:

- Between 6:30 A.M. and 8:00 A.M., the circuits the school
  buses travel every day, which should be avoided during
  those hours.
- The afternoon shift at the factory that lets out at
  4:00 P.M., with a predictable series of roads and intersections clogged for half an hour. Avoid those intersections
  between 4:00 and 4:30, for example.
- That stretch of road where the cross-country team runs
  every afternoon. Point out the times and places where
  they cross the road, and remind her that they probably
  won't strictly obey rights-of-way as they cross.
- The crosswalk just beyond the vision-obstructed curve
  in the road, where bikers, joggers, and dog walkers cross
  at all times of the day. Find a landmark before the curve
  where she should begin braking, in order to be going
  slowly enough to deal with this unpredictable traffic
  when she comes around the curve.
- The spot behind the hedge where the local police hide
  early in the morning with their radar guns. Warn her to
  be especially careful of her speed here.
- The senior center down the block where people totter
  across the pedestrian walkway and some pretty inexplicable merges into traffic happen. Tell her to expect
  cars and seniors to pull out slowly right in front of her
  there.
- The hill where two blind driveways feed onto the road
  just over the crest. Always approach that crest at very
  slow speed, with the foot covering the brake.
- That quarter-mile stretch of wooded area where the deer

cross at dusk. She should keep her peripheral vision sharp, and if she sees one deer, look for others.

- The Woodsons' house six blocks away, with their little Ricky, who likes to turn around in the street with his miniature four-wheeler, followed by his goofy, deaf Labrador. Be especially alert when coming up to this house, and give a wide berth to both Ricky and the dog.

4. Retrace those same routes, this time with your teen driving. Have her repeat as many of the precautions and safety strategies as she can remember. Help her when she misses some. If she hears you say it, thinks about it, then has to repeat it back to you as she drives, you've gone a long way toward hardwiring her awareness and future responses.

14

Staying Found

Time of session: 30 to 60 minutes
Location: Surrounding neighborhood, towns

I take my children everywhere,
but they always find their way back home.
ROBERT ORBEN

Can your teen describe exactly how to get to a frequent destination? My friend Evan Hughes tells this story about one of his daughters: "My daughter Becky was supposed to drive from our church and meet us at a friend's house, maybe ten minutes away. We've driven this same simple route literally hundreds of times before. Well, she went the wrong way on the highway, passed my office, passed several other highways, exits, and towns, and when she finally decided she might have gone too far, she was about 40 miles away. She made it back an hour and a half later. Oh, yeah, she also totaled two cars before she was 18. The only thing I can remember more frustrating than trying to teach her to drive is doing my taxes!"

Many teens can't accurately give directions to their own schools or other places they have been to many times. They've paid little attention to street signs and directions, because they weren't driving. As a driver, your teen will need to know how to receive and give directions, in terms of both street names and landmarks.

When your teen leaves the familiar confines of your nest and moves out into the world, he will drive in many unfamiliar areas. You can make it easier for him by helping to improve his navigational skills. Why would you teach the skills of driving without the complementary skills of navigation? Good drivers know where they are and how they got there. These skills are fine-tuned by paying attention to landmarks and signs, learning to read maps, and, particularly if you're a male, asking for directions.

Neighborhoods are great places to improve your teen's sense of direction while sharpening his visual scan and attention to detail. He now needs to make mental note of street names, distinctive homes, landmarks, intersections, and especially the general direction he's traveling. It's time to get out a detailed local map and prepare to get lost.

1. Get a local map, and review the markings, keys, and geographical directions with your teen.

   A government study called the National Assessment of Educational Progress found that half the country's fourth-graders couldn't accurately identify the Atlantic and Pacific Oceans on a map. These are fairly large bodies of water, by most people's estimation. Fight geographic illiteracy by teaching your teen how to read maps.

   Orient your teen to the location of your home or city on the map, and find familiar streets leading to it. Have him plot and determine the distance to another city using the scale on the map. Then pick out an unfamiliar subdivision or neighborhood where you want to go. Have him determine the best route to get there on the map, and write down each street direction as left, right, or straight: "Left on Maple to Main; right on Main to Oak; right on Oak, and go straight three streets to Washington; then left on Washington."

2. As he drives, help him by calling out the upcoming streets he needs to turn on. When he gets to the chosen location, have him retrace the path he's just taken on the map and then write down the directions to get back home using north, south, east, and west instead of left or right: "West on Maple to Main; north on Main to Oak; east on Oak, and go straight three streets to Washington; then north on Washington."

3. Have him drive back home with these directions, helping to orient him by noting the relative position of the sun or by using major streets or landmarks.

4. When he arrives back home, pick out another spot on the map, preferably in an unfamiliar area. Have him write down the street names and directions to get there using north, south, east, and west, and have him drive to that spot. He should be able to tell by previous turns and/or the position of the sun which general direction he's going each time he turns.

5. Now you're going to get him lost. Have your teen read a book, close his eyes, or otherwise pay no attention to where you're going. (He's had plenty of practice with this.) Then you drive to a nearby place he's never been, making lots of turns to get there. Have him see if he can find where he is on the map, using landmarks, street names, and so on. Even if he can't find the spot, have him drive (without your help) until he finds a street or landmark to orient himself. Help him maintain road awareness as he looks for clues to his location, and make sure he pulls off the road when he needs to consult the map.

It's not just a good idea for your teen to develop his sense of direction and navigational skills. It can also help keep him safe. If he's lost, his attention is diverted from everything else going on around him as he searches for familiar landmarks, signs, and roads. He's more likely to miss important traffic signs and warnings, which could lead to entering exit ramps on freeways, going the wrong way on one-way streets, or ending up in a dangerous neighborhood. These valuable skills seldom get enough attention, and they will help keep your teen from getting lost or into trouble in new and unfamiliar locations.

From this point on, your teen should be responsible for plotting out on a map where you are going to go before each of your driving sessions together, throughout Second, Third, and Fourth Gears.

There's one more bonus to your teen learning how to stay found: he can now be the navigator on family trips, since he can read the tiny print on the maps without squinting or reading glasses.

CHAPTER 15

Vehicle Balance and Following Distance

Time of sessions: 30 to 60 minutes

Location: Rural or lightly traveled road

*Man always travels along precipices . . .
his truest obligation is to keep his balance.*

POPE JOHN PAUL II

One frigid winter afternoon several years ago, I was driving a group of coworkers over a mountain pass from Idaho to Jackson Hole, Wyoming. The road was snowy, but traction wasn't too bad. I was driving a huge Ford Excursion loaded with six passengers and their gear. As I drove uphill, I began a turn around a steep, sharp corner and suddenly came upon an accident scene. Several cars and trucks were stopped dead in the road immediately ahead, and people were just getting out of their cars to warn the drivers coming up the pass. I slammed on the brakes and felt the tires skid as I headed directly toward the truck in front of me. It didn't look as if I was going to be able to stop in time, and I instinctively let off the brakes, hoping that would help stop the skid. That was a mistake, because it shifted the balance of my truck, taking weight off the front tires and reducing their traction.

I then veered toward the shoulder of the road, where I discovered a woman standing next to a huge snowbank, beyond which was a precipitous slope down the mountain. I cranked the wheel the other way and narrowly missed the woman, the snowbank, and the guardrail, then steered back, barely missing the truck I was now alongside, coming to a stop within a foot of it. It all happened within about four seconds. When it was finished, we all exhaled, and my passengers needed to change their underwear.

At that moment, I learned a lot about my driving. I had good instincts and reflexes, but there were things I needed to know about emergency driving situations.

The first was to understand that my truck had an antilock braking system, and I should have continued constant brake pressure as I attempted to steer around the obstacles.

The second was that even though I didn't think I was driving too fast for the conditions, I was. I had missed the crucial "what if" situation: what if I thought I had a reasonable following distance and good traction but came around a blind corner and found a pile-up of vehicles stopped in the middle of the road, with my escape route complicated by a snowbank, a guardrail, a woman, and a steep mountainside?

Finally, I didn't have an instinctive sense of vehicle balance and what affected it. I was driving a very heavy vehicle and lost precious front-wheel traction when I let up on the brakes and shifted all that weight to the rear.

Another second or two of following distance before that blind corner and better understanding of vehicle balance and brake use might have avoided such a close call.

Don't pick an icy mountain road for this exercise. Find a long, lazy rural road, with a number of different types of curves and some long straight stretches. You're going to put the principles of vehicle balance and following distance into practice.

VEHICLE BALANCE

Understanding the basics of vehicle balance isn't that difficult. Here's how to give your teen a firsthand feel for the principles involved:

1. Tell her that a car is essentially a heavy block of metal resting on springs that are attached to the tires, which in turn are connected to the road by four tiny patches of rubber. When the car is stopped, the weight of the block of metal is distributed pretty evenly on those springs and tires.

2. Find a safe stretch of road, and ask her to brake and pay attention to what happens to the mass of the car. Explain that when a car is in motion, braking causes the center of mass to move forward. She should feel forward movement and be pushed against the seat belt. At the same time, have her notice that the hood of the car drops and the rear of the vehicle rises.

3. Have her accelerate, and notice that doing so shifts the center of mass back to the rear. She will feel movement toward the rear and be pushed back in her seat. Now the hood rises and the rear drops, the opposite of braking. To help her remember these two fundamental aspects of balance and weight transfer, have her think about the movement of the front hood of the car, and remember this simple phrase: "Gas up, brake down." (Note: Although the basic principles of balance and weight transfer discussed in this chapter apply for the most part to all types of vehicles, they most accurately apply to *rear-wheel-drive* vehicles. Front-wheel-drive cars act a little differently in some circumstances. For instance, because of the front-wheel traction and the additional weight up front from the drivetrain, when you lift off the gas with a front-wheel-drive car, weight is typically transferred forward rather than backward.)

4. Find an intersection, and have her make a turn while braking, again concentrating on what happens to the mass of the car. She'll notice that when steering is applied, the center of mass transfers to the right or left side of the vehicle. For example, steering right causes the right side to dip and the left side to rise. Stress that these weight transfers and body tilts all have an effect on traction, the ability of those four small patches of rubber to keep her on the road and in control.

5. Describe what typically gets teens in trouble on curves, where they run off the road and crash at far higher rates than older drivers.

Let's say they enter the curve from a straight stretch with a balanced car. What often happens is that they enter the curve at the same speed as the straightaway, which is too fast. Then they get midway through the turn and feel their tires slip, so they hit the brakes. Pretty reasonable response, right? Actually, no. The reason the tires started to slip is that the driver was asking them to do two things at once—maintain traction and change direction—at a speed where it was impossible to accomplish both. What happened with the balance and traction of the car? When the wheel was turned left, the left side of the car dipped and the right side rose. Then, when the driver braked, it caused the center of mass to move forward and load up the front wheels, putting the majority of the downforce and traction on the left front tire. The rear tires, now with less weight, lost traction and started skidding across the road, while the car's back end headed toward the shoulder. Experiencing this, many new drivers brake even harder, which puts even less weight on the rear tires and compounds the skid, and the car ends up spinning around and off the road. This happens all the time, and it's preventable.

6. Explain how disaster could have been avoided on that curve.

As soon as the tires began to slip, the correct move would be to get off the gas immediately. Unless the speed going into the curve is completely excessive, simply easing off the gas and steering through the curve will usually do the trick.

There's another reason getting off the gas and slowing down have such an impact on traction in curves, and it has to do with physics. Because of momentum, the decrease in speed is not directly proportional to the increase in traction. Cutting your speed in half on a curve reduces the force pushing your car in a straight line (and off the road) by a factor of four. In other words, slowing from 50 mph to 25 mph on a curve quadruples your traction, and the sharper the curve, the greater the effect of speed.

7. Have your teen practice basic weight transfer by experimenting a little with braking and letting off the gas at different points in a curve, ensuring that her speed is under control. The point of this exercise is not to push the envelope of traction and end up practicing recovery from a skid or spin. It's to get her to think and feel how vehicle balance changes as weight is transferred, and especially to understand the geometric effect of speed on traction in a curve. Stress these three key points:

   - More than 95 percent of braking should be done *before* entering a curve.
   - As she enters the turn, have her look ahead toward the end of the curve as she steers through it, with the eyes on where the car should be going, rather than the inside or outside lane markers.
   - She should accelerate only when she finishes the arc of the curve and the wheel is turned straight ahead.

FOLLOWING DISTANCE

A number of guidelines have been published regarding safe following distances for automobiles, but there's only one that should be used: keep a three-to-four-second interval between your car and the car in front of you. This assumes dry pavement and otherwise good driving conditions. The interval needs to be increased, often doubled, if these conditions aren't present.

Maintaining a safe following distance is a central part of being crashproof. About a third of accidents are rear-enders. The rest occur in front of you, and there is no better way to avoid crashing into something in front of you than to give yourself plenty of time and room to make adjustments. After your teen has gone through the vehicle-balance exercises and practiced negotiating curves, have her practice recognizing a four-second following distance:

1. Teach her how to determine a four-second following distance. As a vehicle ahead of her passes a fixed object or road landmark, have her begin counting seconds by saying "one one thousand, two one thousand, three one thousand, four one thousand."

2. When the car she's driving passes that spot, have her note the number of seconds it took to reach the spot. That's the following distance she had behind that car.

3. Practice this several times, and she will get an increasingly precise sense of how far a four-second following distance is at a given speed.

4. On the way back home, make sure that she consistently maintains a four-second following distance from the cars ahead of her.

A four-second following distance will allow a driver to steer or brake out of almost every problem immediately ahead, if the road surface has good traction. You'll find that a four-second following distance is probably a lot more than everyone else on the road uses. Just remember, everyone else is not your child. The additional time and distance it will give her to react may be the difference between a close call and a disaster.

The psychology of hammering home the four-second rule is this: since most drivers typically use a one- or two-second following distance, your teen in likely to fudge on her following distance when you're not in the car. The odds are higher that her fudge factor will result in a three-second distance, the minimum needed, if you drill for four. If you drilled her for two or three, it would likely end up one or two.

The other thing a good following distance does is to create a little more peace of mind for the driver. It gives you time to react, and your reflexes don't have to be lightning-quick. If she has a built-in cushion of time and space, she'll be less likely to feel overwhelmed with all the stimuli she's trying to deal with.

Here's the corny phrase to help her remember this: "Follow at four, in bad weather more."

Second Gear Accomplishment Checklist

_____ Forward scans lengthened to a 15-to-25 second lead time, or one-quarter to a half-mile ahead. Can simultaneously monitor traffic signs, signals, road conditions, and other vehicles, bicycles, and pedestrians.

_____ Peripheral scans widened. Head, neck, and eyes move when scanning. Can identify traffic, buildings, and landscape features well off the sides of the road.

_____ Rear scans frequent, using all mirrors and over-the-shoulder glances when necessary.

_____ Practices continual eye movement, shifting and alternating scans between the immediate action, scan and plan, and crashproof ranges.

_____ Estimates closure rates of approaching cars accurately.

_____ Has established closure rate and traffic entry landmarks for most frequent intersections.

_____ Habitually looks left-right-left, then right again, before proceeding at all intersections.

_____ Uses closure rates and allows an adequate gap to enter traffic safely at intersections.

_____ Understands risks and strategies of intersections with lights—red-runner rule, clarity on yellow lights, stop/go points, two-to-three-second hesitation.

_____ Displays understanding of and adherence to all rights-of-way at intersections.

_____ Has mapped out the most hazardous situations and consequent strategies for most frequently driven routes.

_____ Has had an opportunity to give crashproof commentary on your driving.

_____ Can read maps and use all the key information they contain.

_____ Can use a map to get to an identified location and can do so with both left and right as well as north, south, east, and west directions.

_____ Can get found when intentionally lost through use of maps, orienting by driving, and asking for directions.

_____ Understands the principles of vehicle balance, including the effects of acceleration, braking, and steering on weight transfer.

_____ Understands the mistakes many teens make that cause them to run off the road on curves and how to avoid them through proper braking and speed control.

_____ Understands the principles of following distance and consistently maintains a three-to-four-second following distance.

_____ Maintains sustained awareness and focus for up to an hour of driving.

_____ Assumes a defensive driver attitude, expecting other drivers to make mistakes.

Third Gear: Increasing the Challenge

In Second Gear, your teen learned how to expand and refine his visual search and scan skills, and understand the importance of safe following distances. He found out how vehicle balance works, learned how to navigate intersections, and how to read maps and avoid getting lost.

Now it's time for him to put that knowledge to work in more complex circumstances, to integrate the skills and behaviors you've been working on in previous sessions. During Third Gear, he'll drive in the most challenging situations, including busy urban streets, high-speed freeways, and hazardous weather. He or she will learn to successfully share the road with trucks and motorcycles, as well as negotiate the pedestrians, bicycles, and hustle-bustle of the city.

You'll both learn how to stay out of trouble, too, by understanding how to avoid skids, spins, and running off the road, and by practicing how to recover control if those events happen. Finally, your teen will learn to have a master disaster plan for when mechanical failures occur.

Make sure you allow enough time to complete Third Gear. It will likely take several months to expose your teen to varying road and weather conditions, but this is where the critical skills your teen has been developing get put into practice.

CHAPTER

16

Freeway Strategies

Time of session: 30 to 45 minutes

Location: Divided highway

He who hesitates is not only lost, but miles from the next exit.

<small>UNKNOWN</small>

Driving on divided highways is intimidating for many beginning drivers. Traffic is heavier and faster, and there are all those trucks and on- and off-ramps. Collision and fatality rates are actually lower on expressways than on other types of roadways, however, and expressways have a number of other advantages, among them:

- Lack of cross traffic and confusing intersections.
- Head-on crashes less likely because of divided traffic.
- No slow-moving vehicles, pedestrians, or bicycles.
- Wide, paved shoulders for stopping or emergency escape routes.
- Fewer fixed objects near the sides of the road.
- Frequent barriers and fences in animal-crossing areas.
- Large, visible signage.

On the expressway, your teen's forward visual scan needs to lengthen even further, since things approach more quickly at higher speed. His peripheral scan needs to focus on awareness and protection of the zones immediately surrounding his car, rather than the more encompassing peripheral focus needed on urban streets, with their constant side traffic and pedestrians.

Begin your teen's experience with expressway driving at nonpeak times, avoiding rush-hour congestion. Then spend several driving sessions getting your teen comfortable on divided highways, mindful of the following highway strategies.

Go With the Flow, but Speeding Costs Dough

Some beginning drivers are especially hesitant to drive at the 55- or 65-mph speeds of a typical expressway, but it can be dangerous to drive much more slowly than the rest of traffic, hence the posted minimum speeds on many expressways. In general, your teen should try to stay within 5 mph of the speed of the surrounding traffic, in order to cause the least disruption of flow. The reality, however, is that the average speed on many expressways is 10 to 20 mph *faster* than the posted speed limit, and teens can feel pressured to match the speeds of other drivers. It's not easy when everyone is flying past them and annoyed tailgaters cling to their bumpers and flash them the "You're number one" sign with their longest digit. They need to resist the urge to keep up, however, because teens are simply not yet equipped to drive 75 mph, despite how exhilarating (and easy) it is to do.

In addition to the increased braking distance associated with higher speed, there's another element of risk in joining the pack on the freeway. Expressway drivers who are bunched together at higher than the posted speed limit almost always have reduced following distances, usually less than two seconds. Your teen should maintain his four-second following distance, especially on expressways, and that's hard to do unless he's in the far right lane.

Focus on the very tangible issues of expensive tickets and permit or license suspensions to help curb the tendency to speed on the freeway. Many police officers seem inclined to ticket younger drivers aggressively to make a point while they are impressionable. Your teen should understand that it is not a compelling explanation to tell a police officer that he was speeding because everybody else was, and he was just keeping up with traffic. Everybody else may have been, but they caught *him*. And it's going to hurt.

BRAKE LIGHTS: YOUR TEEN'S EARLY WARNING SYSTEM

Teens are always surprised at how quickly traffic can go from 60 mph to 10 mph on an expressway. Many things can suddenly bring a long string of cars to a quick halt, and momentary lapses of attention can cause multiple-vehicle pile-ups in a flash. Your teen must practice swiveling his foot from the gas to cover the brake pedal as soon as he sees brake lights ahead.

It's not the brake lights of the car directly in front of him that's most important, either. If he is scanning traffic a quarter-mile ahead, his foot should be covering the brake pedal well before the brake lights of the car in front of him come on, because he's seen red lights come on far ahead up the highway. He may not end up needing to brake, but he will have saved precious time by covering the brake. If his following distance is adequate—three to four seconds—he will have time to stop if the road is dry.

EXPRESSWAY LANE USAGE

Your teen should stick to the far right lane for most of his initial expressway driving. He will be traveling slower than everyone else anyway, and it will give him a feel for the ebb and flow of expressway traffic without having to make frequent lane changes or deal with tailgaters going 20 mph faster. Lane weavers are endemic on expressways, but most of them flit between the far left and middle lanes in their attempt to stay ahead of the traffic flow. Staying in the right lane will help your teen avoid all but the most dedicated weaverbirds.

Once he gets more comfortable driving on freeways, however, when there are more than two lanes, the middle lane may be the most appropriate one. The benefits of the middle lane include avoiding the speeders in the left lane and the more frequent merging traffic of the far right lane. The middle lane will still have drivers changing lanes into it from both sides, so good mirror use is essential.

Many teens will check their mirrors and five seconds later start to change lanes, only to discover that a car, truck, or motorcycle has sped up from behind them or moved rapidly across a lane and suddenly occupies the lane they were moving into. All three mirrors need to be checked, plus a final over-the-shoulder blind spot check must be done immediately before changing lanes.

ENTRANCE AND EXIT RAMPS

Collisions on limited-access highways frequently occur in the areas immediately before and after interchanges. Staying mostly in the right lane will give your teen lots of practice in dealing with entrance and exit ramps. Once he has established some comfort in simply driving for miles down an expressway, let him practice repeatedly entering and exiting. Have him take the exit ramp, then immediately get onto an entrance ramp and get back onto the highway, repeating this several times as he progresses along the highway. Each on- and off-ramp may present some additional choices for him, and a series of merges on and off the highway in succession is more effective practice than doing one or two each driving session.

If you can, find an urban stretch of freeway that offers a number of different types of interchanges and ramps, such as diamond, trumpet, cloverleaf, weave, and all-directional. If an entrance ramp joins an expressway from the left, he'll need to get fully up to speed even earlier on the ramp, because he will be entering the fastest lane of the expressway instead of the slowest.

In some situations, an entrance ramp can also serve as an exit ramp, with traffic entering and leaving the expressway on a common lane. In this case, the driver entering the highway must yield the right-of-way to the driver leaving the expressway.

YOUR TEEN DOES NOT HAVE THE RIGHT-OF-WAY WHEN ENTERING TRAFFIC.

Many teens assume that they have the legal right-of-way when entering a highway and that other cars are supposed to move over and allow them in. Well, it's great when they do, but they are not required to. Cars already on the highway have the right-of-way, and it's the merging driver's responsibility to signal, find an open spot, and safely merge into traffic. This is where it sometimes gets difficult, and scary, for a teen. Sometimes it appears there just isn't any spot open, and they can quickly panic and try to move into a lane without adequate space, slow down, or even stop at the end of the ramp, an obviously dangerous choice.

The key is to learn to identify potential open gaps in traffic well ahead of when the entrance lane ends, and adjust speed and positioning for the merge. Quick looks over his shoulder while he is on the entry ramp will help him gauge where the merge gaps will be. He must take into account the closure rates of cars approaching him in the lane he wants to merge into and make sure that cars are not moving into his merge lane from other lanes. It's harder to get that kind of visual information from his mirrors, so make sure he also uses over-the-shoulder checks to determine safe entry spots. Repeated practice will quickly develop these skills.

NEVER STOP, BUT ALWAYS HAVE AN ESCAPE ROUTE.

Teens need to recognize the danger of stopping on an entrance ramp. If no merge space is available and they run out of room on the ramp, in most cases the highway shoulder can be an escape route, where they can pull off and wait until a gap opens. Make sure he always notes the following distance of the car behind him on the entry ramp. If he has to pull onto the shoulder, he should know if there are also increased odds of being rear-ended. When he pulls back onto the highway, the gap he's looking for will need to be far larger than in a normal merge, since he will need much more time to get up to highway speed from a dead stop. Where possible, always use the shoulder to build up speed before rejoining the right lane.

ENTER AND EXIT AT HIGHWAY SPEED.

Many beginning drivers are hesitant to accelerate quickly enough on expressway entrance ramps. Care needs to be taken, especially if the ramp is curved, but it's important that your teen get up to highway speed before he merges. If he is traveling at highway speed as he enters traffic, he will be better able to make any position or speed adjustments needed to merge succesfully.

New drivers are also more likely to slow down when approaching an exit ramp. Turn signals should be used well in advance of the exit, with highway speed maintained until he is off the expressway and onto the exit ramp.

THE GOLDEN RULE ON EXPRESSWAYS

Remind your teen how stressful it was when he approached the end of an entry ramp to an expressway and no one moved over to let him in. Since he won't want to put other drivers in that same position, he'll need to give cars entering the freeway ahead of him plenty of room to merge. Teach him to watch for the freeway signs alerting him to upcoming entrance and exit ramps, allowing time to decide whether entering traffic will require him to slow down or move to the middle lane. Automatically moving over a lane when approaching entrance ramps will avoid problems. When he changes lanes make sure that he checks his mirrors and signals well ahead of entering traffic.

PASSING PRACTICE

Head-on collisions, which often involve botched passes, cause more than 5,000 deaths annually and account for nearly 14 percent of all traffic fatalities. Divided highways are the best place to begin teaching passing techniques with your teen, since lane changing and overtaking vehicles can be practiced more safely there. Before he ever attempts to pass a car on a two-lane road, he should practice on a divided highway. The techniques are similar, without the time and space constraints.

When practicing passing on a divided highway, have your teen make sure that all zones around the vehicle are clear with visual and mirror checks, then use his turn signal to communicate a lane change. Have him steer smoothly into the lane to the left. After he has overtaken the car, make sure he can see both of its headlights in his interior rearview mirror before signaling and moving back into the original lane.

Passes should be completed quickly, with as little time as possible spent in the blind spot of the car being passed, so a rule of thumb is to be going a good 10 mph faster than the car he is passing. If that takes your teen more than 5 or 10 mph over the speed limit, he shouldn't make the pass.

On two-way roads, the speed differential is far more critical. Passing on two-way roads should be strongly discouraged with your teen. It's tricky, and he can get into serious trouble very quickly. Unless the road is straight with long sight lines, your teen should attempt passing on two-way roads only when it involves slow-moving vehicles going at least 20 mph below the speed limit.

When he does pass on a two-way road, he will need a 15-mph difference in speed to overtake in a safe manner and in a reasonable time and distance. After he overtakes the vehicle, as on the expressway, make sure he pulls back into the right lane only when he can see both headlights of the passed car in his rearview mirror. If it does not look as if it will be a safe pass—the car he's overtaking speeds up, or an oncoming car appears—he should brake firmly but carefully and slip back behind the car he was attempting to pass. That's a far safer maneuver than speeding up and trying to squeeze in. Likewise, when your teen is being passed on a two-way road, make sure he gets off the gas as soon as the other driver is in the passing lane and only gets back on it when the pass is complete.

One of the most significant skills most teen drivers lack is the ability to determine the time it takes for their vehicle and another coming head-on to meet at a given speed. So it's hard for most teens to comprehend how long it actually takes to make a successful pass. Make sure he understands that if the car he wants to pass is going 50 mph and he starts the pass two seconds behind the vehicle and drives 60 mph, that pass will last more than 20 seconds and take one-third of a mile of road to complete! To reinforce this concept, use the following corny phrase: "When in doubt, don't move out."

Use passing practice on freeways to improve the skills needed to overtake other cars successfully, and set the stage for some limited and cautionary passing practice on two-way roads.

Urban Driving

Time of Session: 30 to 45 minutes

Location: City

*Americans will put up with anything
provided it doesn't block traffic.*

DAN RATHER

Does anyone really enjoy driving in the city? Urban driving is the most stressful kind of driving for most people. It often takes, as Dan Rather might say, courage. Potential hazards are all over the place. Distractions are multiplied, and there's more action, traffic, and noise, requiring concentrated attention and constant scanning. Not surprisingly, crashes that cause injuries and property damage occur at twice the rate in urban areas compared with nonurban areas (although the fatality rate is half that of rural areas). Urban areas are where all of the skills your teen has been learning so far will really pay off, so head into the city for the next couple of driving sessions.

Because urban driving requires such focused awareness, you should again "drive in her shoes" for the first trip into the city. You drive the first time, and have your teen provide the crashproof commentary, verbally identifying all the things you should be seeing as you drive. Then, later in this session or in a future one, have her drive while you provide the commentary. She'll start to adjust her raptor vision and scanning skills to the unique characteristics of an urban environment. In the city, a driver's peripheral scan is usually bounded and restricted by a corridor of buildings. Accordingly, an urban scan needs to be concentrated as follows, in order of priority:

1. *Ahead.* Because of the slower speeds and minimal space between vehicles, more attention needs to be paid to what's directly in front of the driver in the city—the cars ahead, pedestrians crossing, traffic signs and signals. Your teen's sight line and path of travel are largely dictated by what the car right in front of her is doing.

2. *Up.* Overhead signals are a high priority. They govern the intersections, by far the most common areas where urban crashes occur, and need to be perceived and planned for several lights ahead. Remind your teen to be aware of "stale" green lights—those that have been green for some time and are about to turn yellow.

3. *Sides.* Next in importance is what's going on in the periphery. Street signs necessary for navigation will be on both sides. Watch for "snipers," cars that will zoom up beside and dart in front of your teen. Pedestrians, bikes, and pets will enter the street not only at intersections but also from between parked cars and anywhere else it's possible to cross a street. *Always* give pedestrians the right-of-way, whether they're wrong or not.

4. *Behind.* Mirrors must be used to keep track of following traffic, especially vehicles changing lanes and passing your teen.

To reduce confusion on your initial urban driving exercises, you should concentrate on the sides and behind, while your teen concentrates on ahead and overhead, until she can incorporate each into her urban scanning process.

A 1995 Insurance Institute for Highway Safety study of more than 4,500 crashes in four urban areas revealed the most common reasons for crashes in cities. What's especially notable about these crashes is that virtually all of them are preventable, mostly by increased awareness and good visual scanning.

Let's look at the five causes accounting for 75 percent of all crashes and consider how to address each:

- 22 percent involved drivers who ran red lights or other traffic controls such as stop or yield signs.

    As discussed in Chapter 12, a few simple habits will keep your teen out of trouble here. First, assume that someone will run the light or sign, so she should sharpen the peripheral scan when approaching or stopped at an intersection. Second, hesitate two to three seconds after a light has turned green before proceeding into an intersection. Finally, fine-tune her stop/go judgment when approaching intersections, so she doesn't end up going through a yellow that turns red while she's in the intersection.

- 18 percent occurred when a car that was either stopped or in the process of stopping was struck from behind.

    Avoiding being rear-ended by someone else is a bit tricky, because you can't control the vehicle spacing, reaction time, and braking response of the car behind you. Your teen can, however, reduce the odds that she will be rear-ended.

    Be predictable. Maintaining a consistent speed, using turn signals ahead of time, and braking in a smooth, controlled manner make your teen a more predictable driver, less likely to surprise a tailgater or an inattentive driver.

    Be visible. If your teen always keeps her headlights on, she'll not only be more visible to approaching drivers, but the extra brightness of her taillights will help make her more visible to drivers behind her, too. Use brake lights as warning signals, tapping them earlier and more frequently than usual when you are going to slow down or stop.

Don't force others to be good at avoiding rear-ending you. One of the easiest ways to avoid being hit from behind is to avoid pulling out in front of drivers without giving them adequate time and space. It happens every day. Someone pulls out in front of an oncoming car and gets crunched in the back bumper because she either didn't accurately assess the closure rate of the oncoming car or she was in a hurry and cut it too close.

- 14 percent happened when a car ran off the road and struck an object.

Running off the road in an urban environment is most often the result of being distracted and losing focus on immediate driving needs or taking corners too fast. Chapter 15 provides strategies for maintaining balance and control in curves and corners, Chapter 18 focuses specifically on running off the road, and Chapter 26 covers handling distractions in great detail.

- 13 percent involved a vehicle swerving into another occupied lane.

Chapter 11 covers space management and mirror use, to determine which lanes are occupied and have an escape route to use if a swerve or evasive action is needed.

- 9 percent involved motorists turning left and hitting an oncoming vehicle.

Your teen can employ at least three strategies to avoid this type of crash. First, she should ease her car into the intersection a little before attempting to turn left across traffic, so she can execute the turn quickly after identifying a gap in traffic. Second, before turning, she should look though the windshields of cars that pass her through the intersection, to detect small cars or tailgaters that may be hidden behind other cars. Third, make sure she understands all the rights-of-way involved at the intersection.

Speaking of rights-of-way, urban areas have the most issues with them. Who has precedence? Who goes next? As in an argument with your spouse, you may be right, but the point is to get out of the situation without bloodshed. It's important for your teen to understand all the rules and etiquette of rights-of-way on the road. For a crashproof driver, however, it's equally important to understand that just because you have the legal right-of-way doesn't mean it will be acknowledged or respected. Rights-of-way are frequently misunderstood or ignored in the city. It doesn't do a whole lot of good to know that you had the right-of-way when you've just been sideswiped by someone else who either didn't know or didn't care. When driving in the city, reinforce the reality of rights-of-way with this reminder: "Regarding rights-of-way, you are right when you stay out of everyone's way."

The data on city crashes dictate the solutions for avoiding them. By watching for red-light or stop-sign runners, giving adequate warning time when braking, staying in her own lane, and being careful when making left-hand turns at intersections, your teen should be able to reduce her likelihood of an urban crash by about 75 percent.

Other city characteristics that require specific attention:

- Buses and taxis assume a right-of-way when they pull out from a curb.
- Garbage, construction, delivery, and other commercial trucks double-park with impunity, and their drivers shuttle back and forth across the street with various loads.

• Pedestrians assume the right-of-way at any time and any place and can be expected to cross the street suddenly from any point.
• Bicyclists, especially messengers, can be worse than pedestrians. They're faster, in more of a hurry, ignore even more traffic rules, and can quickly slide into your blind spots seemingly from out of nowhere.

Navigation skills and a good sense of direction are also important in the city. It's easy to get completely turned around among the bridges, tunnels, one-way streets, confusing or missing street signs, and construction detours. Keep the radio off, and have your teen plot out her trip beforehand with more detail than usual. This is where she'll make the most use of the skills learned in Chapter 14. You'll still need to give her lots of navigation help in the city. And when you're both hopelessly lost, stop for something to eat, and ask a local where the heck you are.

CHAPTER 18

Running Off the Road
(and Returning Safely)

Time of session: 30 to 45 minutes
Location: Country road

Stuff happens.
Bumper sticker (modified)

More than half of all teen vehicle fatalities occur when a car goes off the road and rolls over or crashes into something. A variety of things can cause this—swerving to avoid an object, drifting off the road surface as a result of inattention, sleepiness, slippery conditions, or speeding, for example. Running off the road is a dangerous situation by itself, but most drivers compound this with either a complete lack of any response or too much or too little steering or braking.

Here's what typically happens, with the end result too often a vehicle rollover:

- Vehicle goes off the road on the right shoulder.
- Driver brakes, causing skidding and/or weight loading on the wheels off the road.
- Driver compensates by yanking the steering wheel hard to the left, shooting the car back onto the road, and rocking the vehicle's weight hard onto the right wheel.

• Driver compensates again by yanking the wheel hard to the right to get back to the original lane and rocks the weight back onto the opposite wheels, this time with enough accumulated force to cause the vehicle to flip over and roll.

Reduce the odds that your teen will react similarly in such a situation by following the game plan below for the day's driving session.

Find an infrequently traveled road where there is a difference in shoulder composition or a definite drop-off between the road surface and the shoulder. Make sure that the drop-off is no more than about four inches. (Be aware that steering back up onto a hard edge can do damage, usually invisible, to a tire. Make sure that your teen is going as slowly as possible when driving back onto the road.)

Pick a long, straight stretch of the road where the shoulder is wide and there are no obstacles or hazards anywhere near the road. Choose a time with the least heavy traffic, say Sunday at 7:00 A.M. or Saturday at 2:00 P.M. Now you're going to drive in their shoes again. Get behind the wheel yourself first, and demonstrate how to run off the road and return safely by doing the following:

1. With no traffic ahead or behind you, drive slowly off the road, at about 10 mph, until the two outside tires are off the main road surface. Make sure your feet are off both the brake and the accelerator.

2. Steer gently to align the car parallel with the edge of the road, keeping the tire edges off the road edge.

3. If the area ahead is clear, brake carefully, ease the other two wheels off the roadway, and come to a stop.

4. If the area ahead is not clear and you must return to the roadway, check oncoming and following traffic, and steer gently, with only a little turning, to get two wheels at a time back on the road.

5. As soon as the first tire is back on the road surface, countersteer gently in the other direction, then steer back gently toward the road again to get the remaining wheels on the road.

The most important point is to avoid steering to get all four wheels back on the road in the same maneuver.

Repeat this exercise at gradually increasing speeds as your comfort and technique develop, up to a maximum of about 35 mph if all conditions allow. Then have your teen follow the same exercises, as you vocalize each step as it happens, to reinforce the sequence:

"All right now, ease it *gently* off the road, no brakes or accelerator, but only until you get the two outside wheels off the road."

"Good. Now steer *gently* to bring the car parallel to the road, keeping the other two wheels on the road."

"There. Now brake carefully, and ease the other two wheels off the road. OK, now steer straight ahead, and come to a stop."

To practice the situation where he must return to the road while rolling, after bringing the car parallel to the edge of the road, guide him through this sequence to get back on the highway safely:

"OK, now you're going to *gently* turn the wheel to the *left* until you feel the *first* wheel get back on the road. There it is. Now gently turn the wheel back to the right, and straighten the car up a little."

"Good. Now steer again *gently* to the *left* until the outside wheels get on the road. There—now steer gently back to the right, and straighten it toward the middle of the lane."

This can be controversial. Driving instructors are not typically trained in emergency braking technique, so they don't practice it with their students. Some may contend that this exercise is risky. But here, again, are the statistics: 50 percent of all fatalities occur when a car goes off the road. It's reasonable to conclude that a substantial percentage of those fatalities happen because no one gets trained in how to react correctly when a car leaves the road.

Your teen *will* at some point in his driving career encounter a situation where he will go off the road surface. The steps outlined above can and should be practiced, and if done correctly is not needlessly risky. There's no other way to make the responses instinctive and automatic.

Practicing this will highlight several valuable skills for your teen. He'll know that going off the road does not necessarily mean going out of control. He'll understand the sensation of forcing himself to leave the road surface without braking, which is counterintuitive. He'll feel how much steering-wheel turn it takes to bring only two wheels at a time onto a road surface.

You can't afford to hope that your teen will happen to do these things correctly in a crisis situation. You can help to ensure that he does by practicing them. You can do it. And so can he.

CHAPTER
19

Skids and Spins

Time of session: 30 to 45 minutes
Location: Slippery parking lot or frozen lake

*When teen drivers lose control of a car, it's pretty predictable.
Their feet start doing "Riverdance" on the pedals,
and their arms flail and spin on the steering wheel like there's
a bee in the car. It would be funny if it weren't so scary.*

JEFF PAYNE, PRESIDENT, DRIVERS EDGE

Laurie Reed, who with her husband, Randy, has helped four teen-agers learn to drive, vividly remembers taking her first icy spin in a car: "The winter I was fifteen, Dad took me to the parking lot of the high school, after school hours or on weekends. There was always plenty of snow and ice covering the pavement, and he put me through my paces. Getting the car up to speed, Dad would hit the brakes and force the car into a skid. He handled it with ease, thus demonstrating for me the 'controlled skid.' Again and again I practiced with him in that lot until I felt confident enough to tackle some of the lesser-traveled country roads near our home. Those lessons were priceless. Living in Michigan, I have had ample opportunities over the years to use what I learned that winter. Dad passed away nine years ago, but each time I encounter icy conditions, I think of him and send a silent thank you."

Understanding why skids and spins happen, knowing how to avoid them, and—in the worst case—knowing how to recover from them can help keep your teen crashproof. This session is harder to practice, but it's possible. Snowy, icy, or rain-slicked vacant parking lots or frozen lakes can be used to practice recovery from skids and spins. These venues have their own additional hazards, of course—hitting light posts or crashing through the ice, for example—so choose with care. The good news is that many people can develop an instinctive and correct skid-control response after only a couple of slides.

A front-wheel skid occurs when a car experiences "understeer," and there isn't enough traction on the front tires. This typically occurs when steering though a curve or corner, especially if it is approached too fast. In a front-wheel skid, traction has been shifted to the sidewalls of the front tires from the treads, making it impossible to develop turning force. Meanwhile, the rear wheels keep pushing the vehicle forward, so the car tends to move straight ahead, away from the intended travel path, even though the driver may continue to turn the steering wheel.

In a rear-wheel skid, the car experiences "oversteer" when the rear wheels lose traction and the front of the car points left or right of the travel path without steering input in that direction. This typically occurs on a slick surface with excessive speed, compounded by braking or sudden steering movements, and can result in a car rotating 180 degrees or spinning if not quickly corrected.

1. Find your empty, slippery parking lot or frozen lake (with several feet of ice minimum). Have your teen get up to 20 or 25 mph and brake hard. When the front or back end starts to skid, have her immediately get off the accelerator and concentrate on looking and steering in the direction she wants the car to go. This is the first step, training her foot to get off the gas and training her eyes on where she wants the front of the car to end up.

2. Make sure she resists the urge to brake when the car starts to skid (especially if the car does not have antilock brakes), because she may lose steering control if she brakes. As she slows down and regains traction, have her steer (gently) back to the direction she wants the front of the car to go. After regaining steering control in a front-wheel skid, she may need to touch the brakes gently to shift some weight onto the front wheels.

Most newer cars today have antilock brakes, and depending on the circumstances, she may be able to brake carefully as she regains steering control with small, careful wheel movements. However, the most important thing is to regain steering control, and light, progressive acceleration can often help return rear-wheel traction by shifting weight back onto the rear wheels.

3. Reinforce that the hands follow the eyes. Many drivers have been confused with the common advice to "steer into" the skid. To make it simple, tell your teen that if her car begins a rear-wheel skid, she should look in the direction she wants to go and steer in that direction. Her hands will follow her eyes. (Teens more frequently end up with rear-wheel skids. In both rear- and front-wheel skids, she should gently steer in the opposite direction from where the front end is heading.)

4. Practice getting into gentle skids several times, until your teen gets a feel for the correct sequence to follow and understands how to make proper (gentle) steering corrections, depending on whether the front end or the rear end is skidding.

5. Emphasize to your teen that in a skid, most drivers' hands are too late and their correction too great. When correcting for a skid, countersteer quickly but with only a modest wheel

throw. Remember this with "In a skid, hands are quick, steering's a flick," and its corollary, "The higher the speed, the less correction you need."

Spins are a lot trickier and much more dangerous. Skids that are not corrected in time can become spins, or a car can immediately end up in a spin without the prequel of skidding if the speed and conditions are right. In either case, a spin means that control has been lost. Some people freeze up in a spin, watching in a state of shock as the landscape whooshes past. The second a car starts to spin, however, you must immediately grip the wheel tightly, get off the gas, and work to maintain steering control. In most situations, braking during a spin increases your risk. Steering control must be regained and the car pointed straight before braking can be safe and effective.

Advanced driving schools are safer places for your teen to learn what happens when a car skids and how to correct it, but this should be considered only with a great deal of thought and caution. More information on this subject can be found in Chapter 29.

The absolute best way for your teen to deal with skids and spins is never to get into one.

CHAPTER 20

Professional Racing Techniques: 10 Tips to Help Crashproof Your Teen

There are two things no man will admit he cannot do well: drive and make love.

STIRLING MOSS, LEGENDARY RACER

Have you ever dreamed about being a professional racer? Of course you have. But something's been holding you back. Perhaps the prospect of smashing into a concrete wall at 230 mph has something to do with it.

This chapter isn't about how to go really fast—it's about keeping out of trouble on the road. Professional racers use a variety of techniques to stay alive on the track, and your teen can effectively incorporate many of them in his driving.

The following story, courtesy of Alan Siderov, is illustrative: "I was driving a prototype Ferrari on a racetrack. In turn one, at about 160 mph, the outside rear tire exploded. It was instantaneous and took out the suspension on that side plus half the bodywork. I have never, before or since, had a car try to spin out as violently. What saved me was not dazzling skill, wit, or good table manners. It was a nagging internal voice yelling, 'Don't look at the wall, look toward turn two.' This was a good half-mile away, and if I replay the scene, I can still see the tire-blackened asphalt in the distance. The car slid, twisted, and slid some more while I worked like an amateur goat wrestler. When I got the car stopped, it was a paper's width from the wall. Had I even glanced at that barrier during the slide, I would have missed the only information of use, where I wanted the car to go. I've sat with thousands of drivers of all ages on the skid pad and the racetrack, and when things get hectic, it is the correct use of eyesight that fails first. This is usually accompanied by random pedal applications, like a confused pianist. Sooner or later, just about every driver, no matter how cautious and attentive, will find themselves in a situation where danger looms. It's good to be ready for that moment with something less inane than 'Steer into the skid and pump the brakes.' The eyes have it."

Some of the techniques below have been touched on in earlier chapters, but the concepts are important enough to reemphasize. Here are ten ways to help improve your teen's (and your own) driving skill and safety odds, from the collective experience and wisdom of professional racers.

1. Search far down the track.

Competitive drivers focus their eyes way down the track, in order to process the conditions ahead quickly and react instantly. Our minds can process data well ahead of when our bodies actually need to do something. It's much like good downhill skiers—their minds are always processing the turns that are four to five turns downhill from the one their legs are actually navigating.

Beginning drivers normally train their eyes on the road at a point much too close to the front of their car. Ask your teen at various times to pinpoint the area on the road ahead where his vision is concentrated. Then have him practice focusing 2 to 3 times further down the road, enabling him to steer with fewer corrections, sharpen his peripheral vision, and react to traffic conditions ahead much more quickly.

Ask your teen periodically about something you see way down the road to test whether he is incorporating this visual technique. He'll need continual practice at first, because he may revert back to his initial focal spots unless you remind him until it becomes a habit.

2. Look where you want to go, not at what you want to avoid.

In racing lingo, this is known as target fixation. For example, you are in the middle of a turn, you lose traction, and your car heads for the edge of the road. If you look at the guardrail you are about to hit, you increase the likelihood that you will steer into it. Racers know to resist that urge and focus their vision (and thus their steering) on where they want the car to go instead.

Some professional racing instructors estimate that at least 20 percent of male and 10 percent of female drivers have a tendency toward target fixation. This can be especially applicable to common road situations. Police officers, firefighters, rescue workers, and road-repair crews are well aware of this phenomenon. Disabled cars on the side of the road, orange traffic cones, road-repair signs, guardrails—all can be potential unwitting targets for drivers who fixate on the object they are trying to avoid.

When negotiating a curve or a corner, look to the *inside* of the curve. Watch racers in action—their heads will actually lean into the inside of the curve, following their eyes.

Look where you want to go, not where you want to avoid.

3. Steer small.

Beginning drivers tend to make exaggerated steering-wheel movements, especially in a crisis, with too much wheel turning back and forth. Racers know that small, infrequent steering-wheel movements work best. In addition, the higher the speed, the smaller the movement needed. Teens get into trouble when they enter a turn too fast and turn the steering wheel to the same degree they did in a previous turn going much slower.

On the highway, with no traffic in either direction, have your teen practice different amounts of wheel turn at various speeds, being careful to stay within his lane. He will be amazed at what a difference it makes at 55 mph versus 30 mph. The point to be reinforced is that at highway speed, it takes only a couple of seconds of inattention or incorrect steering to be heading toward disaster.

Steering small is especially important when recovering from running off the road, as discussed earlier. Most rollovers happen when two consecutive steering compensations in opposite directions are made with too much wheel turn. To regain control and a straight-ahead bearing, a driver must make limited wheel adjustments, wait a moment for the car to change direction, then make another limited adjustment. Steer small to stay out of trouble.

4. It's often them, not you.

Many crashes that injure professional racers and destroy cars are caused by other drivers, through either an error or an equipment malfunction. The best drivers avoid crashes by watching out for everyone else on the track.

The same is true on the highway. Your teen's awareness of other drivers, especially those ahead of him, is critical to avoiding a crash. Too high a percentage of drivers on the road fall into these categories:

- Teenage boys impersonating Dale Earnhart, Jr., at Daytona.
- Teenage girls applying makeup while talking on the phone and fiddling with the radio.
- Senior citizens with impaired hearing, vision, and memory.

- Businessmen and women with five martinis and a bad attitude because they just lost the Steinberg account.
- Mothers wiping off their toddlers while mentally juggling doctor appointments, school functions, and shopping lists.

The alert, unimpaired, courteous driver obeying all traffic laws will be in the silver Ford Taurus with the headlights on.

Give speeders, weavers, road-ragers, incompetents, and lunatics a wide berth, and you'll avoid much of the mayhem they will inevitably cause.

5. Brake into turns, accelerate out of them.

Many accidents happen on curves, where teens fail to take into account the physics of turning and traction. When a tire changes direction, as in a curve, it incurs extra stress and flex, as the straight-ahead momentum changes to a diagonal momentum. The tire simply can't maintain the same traction while turning at a given speed that it can while going straight at that speed. So virtually all braking should be done in the straightest possible line.

In addition, braking shifts the weight of the car forward and onto the front wheels. Braking before entering a curve not only helps the tires maintain enough traction for the directional change but it also loads the front wheels to give them better traction as the curve is negotiated. When you are past the apex (midway point), acceleration reloads the weight on the rear wheels, providing extra traction where it's needed as you come out of the curve.

6. Smarter beats speedier.

It doesn't matter how fast you were getting there if you never get there. In 2003, a young professional NASCAR racer named Matt Kenseth didn't win a single race. He did, however, win the prestigious Winston Cup Series, pocketing millions of dollars and garnering worldwide acclaim. He did it by consistently finishing in the top ten of almost every race he entered, emphasis on *finishing*. In racing, the fastest guy on the track doesn't necessarily win. Winners attend to the needs of their cars, avoid crashes, and finish by driving smarter than everyone else.

Many tragic accidents are caused because someone was behind schedule, impatient to get somewhere, or cutting corners on common sense. In addition to the safety factor, the reality is that with traffic the way it is virtually everywhere today, very little is gained by going faster than the flow of traffic.

You can see this every day on the highway. Take note of the next car that passes you. You'll usually find him several miles down the road, impatiently riding someone else's bumper, burning more gas, raising his blood pressure, and not getting there any faster than anyone else.

7. Feel your wheels.

Professional racers have to learn how to feel when their car is right and when it's not. They don't have to be expert mechanics or even be able to diagnose everything perfectly. They do need to know, however, through sensory feedback—sound, smell, handling, steering, braking—when something needs attention. Your teen should also learn the feel of his vehicle. He should learn to feel how a car's suspension typically handles sharp turns and minor bumps, how the engine normally sounds when it's warming up and when it's accelerating hard. The amount of foot pressure the brakes need and their stopping distance are good indicators of their safety and condition.

He also needs to tune into how these things change as conditions change—for example, how they are different with a car full of people compared with an empty one. It's not necessarily intuitive to a beginning driver that with luggage in the trunk and four people in the car, he will have to accelerate harder to enter a busy highway and brake more firmly to slow down at the same rate as with an empty car.

It's important to have your teen drive as many different cars as possible—your minivan, your spouse's SUV, your brother's sports car, your mother's sedan. All are instructive. Your teen doesn't need to know much about the specific differences in the mechanical properties of each car, but the more experience he has in quickly assessing a given car's condition and operating personality, the safer and more versatile a driver he will become.

8. React rapidly.

Quick reflexes and rapid decision making are the hallmarks of great racers, even more than sheer technical driving skill. Racers don't have time to agonize over a decision on the track. They have to make the decision *now,* and it needs to be the right one nine times out of ten.

This is where your teen's youthful reflexes come into play and where the payoff may come from all those years of hand-eye practice and decision making he's honed on video games. It's also where the critical benefits of repetition become clear. If he's practiced ten times that when avoiding an object in an emergency braking situation he stomps and steers, he'll be far less likely to spend precious seconds thinking about whether to pull off the road, swerve into the other lane, or keep going and hope it all works out.

9. Take it seriously.

Racers know that every time they get behind the wheel, they are about to engage in a high-risk activity. This is exactly how your teen should feel every time he gets behind the wheel. This doesn't mean be fearful, it means take it seriously. Racers know that it can all end in a second with one unfortunate misjudgment or error. So they prepare, and they respect every other driver on the track. Sponsors, mechanics, fans, and family all count on them to be both skillful and safe.

Make sure that your teen knows that in addition to granting him one of his first tastes of adult responsibility and freedom, you are also counting on him to be both skillful and safe.

10. Speeding stays at the track.

You don't often see professional racers getting ticketed for speeding when they're off the racetrack. Granted, if you had the chance to go 200 mph in a finely tuned machine all the time, you probably wouldn't feel the need to get the Accord screaming. But when professionals speed on the track, they know what they're doing. When amateurs speed on the highway, it's a different story.

CHAPTER 21

Hazardous Driving Situations

Time of sessions: 30–60 minutes
Locations: Various

Never drive faster than your guardian angel can fly.
UNKNOWN

When I was 16, my mother got a brand new company car, and she let me take it out on a date the first night she had it. I went "parking" with my girlfriend on an icy dirt road between two fields in a rural area. Later, backing out, my right rear tire slipped on an icy patch, and the back end of the car slid off the road and over the edge of a drainage ditch, impaling the car's passenger door on a protruding chunk of metal from the drain culvert and nearly giving my girlfriend a heart attack.

The car was hopelessly stuck, and it took two hours for a tow truck to lift it off the metal. When it did, there was a gaping hole the size of a basketball in the door. It took a lot of allowance to cover the insurance cost of fixing that hole. Later that year, I had another bizarre car incident with the same girlfriend, and I stopped seeing her shortly thereafter. Bad car juju.

Teen drivers have more control than they assume in hazardous weather conditions. It's common to blame slippery roads or reduced visibility for a crash. An icy road has never caused a crash, nor has fog.

Drivers have caused crashes because they failed to compensate for the effects of an icy or foggy road.

The first poor choice is to drive in dangerous conditions. Many trips can be avoided or postponed. The second is to drive too fast or too inattentively in dangerous conditions. The third is not to take into account all the other bozos on the road who are violating the first two.

Driving in any kind of hazardous condition—bad weather, decreased visibility, poor traction—requires the same four basic responses:

1. Decreased speed.
2. Increased following distance from the cars in front of you.
3. Heightened vigilance, especially for others' mistakes.
4. More careful braking.

Your teen will seldom get into trouble driving in hazardous situations if she observes these principles and the unique cautions of each condition.

RAIN

It's easy to underestimate the risks of driving on wet roads, although it requires the same caution and response as driving on ice- or snow-covered roads. Stopping distances can double on wet roads. At 50 mph, a dry road will require 175 feet to stop, but when it's wet, it could require more than 350 feet.

Many teens assume that roads are the most treacherous in a pouring rain, but they're actually most slippery during a light rain or mist, when the moisture mixes with highway oil and grime to produce a slick, greasy surface. Heavy rains tend to wash the oil and dirt away, but they present another risk: hydroplaning. When a car hydroplanes, its tires are actually riding on a thin film of water rather than the road surface, and loss of control can occur quickly. If your teen's car starts to hydroplane, she must take her foot off the gas and maintain steering control. With antilock brakes, she can combine this with moderate braking.

With any amount of moisture on the road, the fundamental rules of safe driving in hazardous conditions again apply: slow down, increase the following distance, and brake more slowly and cautiously.

SNOW AND ICE

Snow and ice on the surface of the road create a different set of conditions almost every time, depending on many factors. Teach your teen to be wary where ice forms first—bridges, overpasses, shady spots, windy spots—wherever the warming effects of the earth are reduced. Intersections also tend to have more ice on the road surface, because vehicle exhaust has heated, melted, and reiced the pavement. Slow down well before the intersection in icy conditions.

Traction and braking conditions should be tested before entering high-traffic areas, by carefully applying the brakes at slightly increasing speeds in an area without cars or obstacles. Sometimes the grip is surprisingly good; other times it's deceptively poor.

In very cold conditions, the snow will often be tiny dry flakes that swirl in clouds but don't stick to road surfaces. This type of snow tends not to affect traction as much as visibility. If it's cold enough for this kind of snow, however, chances are that the road surface itself is frozen and very slippery.

Warmer conditions produce heavier, stickier snow. In addition to reducing visibility, this kind of snow can produce several treacherous conditions. During the day, it can pile up and turn roads slushy. At night, crusty ice forms, especially in the packed-down tire lanes. Your teen can hear and feel the difference among hardpack snow, heavy slush, and frozen crust. Heavy slush will slow her down markedly but provide better traction, because the road surface is not frozen. Packed snow provides less tire resistance but poorer traction and conditions ripe for skidding. The crunch and vibration of crusty ice actually provide a little better traction than smoother ice or packed snow, but braking on it can be very unpredictable.

When driving in snow, the traction is always better in the ruts—the tracks worn by the heavier tire traffic in the center of the lanes. Changing lanes across these ruts is very challenging and should be avoided. If she must change lanes, she should do it very slowly and smoothly, with a firm grip on the wheel. It's best to stay in the right lane in these conditions. Let the gamblers test the edge of the envelope in the left lane. No one's getting there any faster in these conditions, anyway. You'll find many of the left-laners farther down the road, spun out in the median or off the road.

Be especially careful of conditions that can lead to "black ice"—high humidity or recent precipitation followed by rapidly decreasing temperatures. Black ice will tend to have a dark sheen, unlike whiter, crusty snow and ice. One key indicator of black ice is that the road noise suddenly ceases. If this happens, get off the gas instantly. At night especially, it's nearly impossible to see black ice ahead of time, and if you hit a patch, you are pretty much out of control and at the mercy of the gods. Always get off the gas immediately if you hit a patch of black ice— even antilock brakes won't help you.

FOG

Foggy conditions are exceptionally dangerous and should be avoided whenever possible. If driving in fog is necessary, the peripheral scan becomes more secondary to the forward scan than usual, because of limited side visibility and the importance of concentrating on the road directly ahead.

Fog causes the high beams on headlights to scatter too much light back at you, actually decreasing visibility, so the headlights should always stay on dim and be accompanied by the fog lights. Pump the brakes to give a brake-light alert to following drivers much farther ahead of a stopping point than you normally would. Some recommend putting the emergency flashers on, to give more visible notice to drivers approaching from behind; others discourage this, and it is illegal in some states.

Turn the radio off and crack the windows so you can hear sounds such as brakes locking up and cars colliding.

The most important thing to do in fog is to reduce driving speed enough to compensate for the reduced forward visibility. If there is more than one lane going in your direction, stay in the right lane. Leave the left lane open for any lunatics with a death wish. If you can't maintain at least a 30-mph speed without outrunning your dimmed headlights, get off the road—the risk of a rear-end collision is too great.

DRIVING AT NIGHT

Nearly 40 percent of teen fatalities occur at night, especially weekend nights. Night driving combines multiple risk factors:

- *Reduced visibility.* Lane markers and road signage are more difficult to see at night for everyone. Landmarks that aid in judging speed, distance, and closure rate are invisible, and to compound this, some people have much poorer night vision than day vision. Despite all this, most drivers do not reduce their speed or following distances at night accordingly. Staying within the speed limit and adhering to at least a four-second following distance are even more important for your teen at night.

   Since peripheral vision is sharply reduced, have your teen concentrate more fully on the forward scan, tracking everything possible to be seen within the confines of the headlight beams—other headlights, taillights, movement, or reflecting eyes on the shoulder.

- *Glare from oncoming headlights.* Don't look directly at headlights coming toward you for more than a couple of seconds at a time. To cope with headlight glare from oncoming vehicles, have your teen periodically scan back and forth from the right edge of the roadway to the center of the road, giving her eyes a break from having to adjust to the intensity of the oncoming headlights. Maintain your lane position by aligning with the lane marker on the right edge of the road, rather than the center line.
- *Increased animal activity.* See Chapter 26 for how to deal with animals on the highway.
- *Loaded drivers.* Far more drivers are under the influence of alcohol and other mind-altering substances at night than during the day, especially on weekends. Watch for erratic driving by those in front of you or oncoming, such as inconsistent speeds or crossing over the center lane and correcting back into a lane.
- *Increased risk with passengers.* With reduced visibility, it's even more important for your teen to maintain concentration. The addition of passengers, especially other teens, can be even more dangerous at night than during the day.
- *Night-vision problems.* Make sure you know whether your teen's night vision is markedly inferior to her daytime vision.

To reduce the risks of night driving, have your teen get accustomed to the challenges it presents by making short, frequent nighttime driving trips with you. Limit any night driving until your teen has displayed competence in almost every driving situation during the day. Be especially careful of night driving before your teen is 17 or has 80 to 100 hours of supervised driving with you.

PERSONAL SAFETY ON THE ROAD

Driving a car not only provides increased autonomy, but it can also increase vulnerability, especially for young women. Personal safety precautions now need more attention, along with a heightened sensitivity to locations, behaviors, and situations conducive to various kinds of human predators. Kristin Backstrom, founder of Safe Smart Women, a driving safety and education firm, offers a dozen tips for staying safe on the road and in the car:

1. BE CAUTIOUS WHEN PULLED OVER BY AN UNMARKED POLICE CAR.

Police in marked cars will almost always use flashing lights and often a siren or loudspeaker when they pull you over, and they will usually flip their interior dome light on when they stop. Unmarked or off-duty police may not, and you should ask to see a badge and picture identification, with your door locked and the window cracked. If you are still suspicious, call 911, and have the local or state police verify the ID or send a marked car.

2. INTENSIFY YOUR AWARENESS OF SURROUNDINGS.

Scan parking lots before parking to identify loiterers. Take note if your car seems to be followed by another car for an unusually long time. Minimize the use of cell phones or portable music devices in potentially unsafe areas because they can distract your attention. Look for the existence and position of security guards or parking attendants. Make strong eye contact with potential predators, letting them know that you're empowered and aware and can identify them. Send out strong vibes that you're keenly aware of what's happening around you.

3. Be cautious about receiving and offering help.

Although it may well be your first instinct to offer help to someone who appears to need it, keep the danger radar on high. That car with the hood up may or may not be disabled. Call 911 to make sure help arrives. The guy asking for spare change may want more than that.

When someone else offers to help you, the same conditions apply. Trust your gut when it comes to helping or being helped.

4. Lock up.

Your doors should be locked not only whenever you park but also when you drive. Carjackings happen.

5. Give yourself a gap.

Leave at least a full car length between you and the car in front of you at traffic lights, stop signs, and intersections. That may give you an escape route if needed.

6. Park smart.

Always park in well-lit lots. Avoid the outskirts of a lot at night and any areas with obstructed visibility. Back in to your parking spot so that you can pull straight out when you're leaving. Don't fumble in your pocket or purse next to your parked car. Have your keys in hand and ready to go as you approach it. Scan the areas surrounding your car before you enter or exit it, and check the backseat before getting in.

7. VARY YOUR ROUTINE.

Predators may follow, track, and study the routines of their intended prey. Vary the times and routes you take when you bike, run, and walk. Use the gym at different times and days. Take different routes to work and back. Park in varying spots.

8. MAKE A LOT OF NOISE IF THREATENED.

Buy a personal attack alarm (or pepper spray). Scream at the top of your lungs. Lay on the horn. Set off the car alarm.

9. TAKE ELEVATORS INSTEAD OF STAIRWELLS.

Stairwells are easy places for predators to hide or lurk. If someone on or entering an elevator makes you nervous, get off immediately. Trust your first instinct.

10. MAKE SURE THAT BUMP WASN'T PLANNED.

One successful tactic used by criminals to get to a vehicle or its occupant is to crunch into the car's fender, usually at low speed. If you're afraid a fender bender was intentional, stay in your locked car, and call 911 immediately.

11. SACRIFICE A TIRE OR A RIM.

If you have a flat tire or a blowout in an obviously dangerous area or congested part of the freeway, keep driving to an exit, a gas station, or some other safer place. Although not recommended, your car can be driven on its wheel rims if necessary. Your tire is probably already toast, and wheels can be replaced.

12. AVOID IT, GIVE IT UP, OR FIGHT.

If you're accosted, the best first option is to run and run hard, scream-ing all the way. (Guys, you can use a manly roar, like the one you give your favorite sports team.) Kick off your shoes, and go fast.

If you can't escape, then you need to give them whatever they want, if it's material goods or money. No possession you have with you or in the car is worth risking your life for.

If you are assaulted physically, fight hard, fight mean, and fight nasty. Scratch eyes, punch throats, knee groins, kick knees, and stomp on feet. Bite. Use a tire iron, chains, or a shovel from the trunk if you can. There are no rules here except to hurt the attacker, the quicker and the harder the better.

FATIGUE

Fatigue is a major contributor to teen auto crashes. Studies have shown that teens who get less than six hours of sleep each night are nearly three times more likely to be in a crash than those who get more than six hours of sleep. Be aware if your teen has had a recent series of short nights or has a chronic sleep deficit. Enforce a reasonable curfew, espe-cially on weekends, and make sure she gets enough sleep.

Watch for signs of fatigue if your teen spends more time on long, open stretches of divided highway and begins driving at night. The rel-ative lack of visual stimuli in both situations can dull the attention and in some cases induce a trancelike state of mind.

To combat fatigue while driving, have your teen try these tricks:

KEEP YOUR MOUTH IN MOTION.

Chewing, swallowing, singing, and talking help keep the mind alert. Eat candy, chocolate, peppermint, or licorice. Chew gum. Drink cold water, coffee, or sodas with caffeine. Sing along with the radio, or argue with the talk-radio guy you love to hate. Keep a conversation running about something you're passionate about. If you're alone, have the argument with yourself. Out loud.

SHOCK YOUR SYSTEM.

Keep the window down and the air rushing through the car. There's a slight possibility that some fatigue could be caused by low-level carbon-monoxide poisoning. Be aware of its accompanying symptoms in addition to drowsiness: headache, dizziness, and nausea. Keep the air conditioner blasting at the same time. Pinch your thigh, or give your face a slap. Turn up the volume on the radio.

KEEP YOUR BLOOD PUMPING.

Part of the fatigue that affects drivers can be caused by lack of circulation after sitting on your behind for long periods. Keep your blood moving—wiggle your toes; squeeze the steering wheel; flex your thighs, glutes, and biceps; stretch your neck; clench your abdominals; and throw back your shoulders. Breathe deeply and exhale forcefully through your mouth. Pull off the road, and walk briskly for a few minutes. Change your position in the driver's seat frequently.

The first sign of fatigue is usually decreased frequency of mirror checking. Pay attention to your teen's eye movements and scanning, and remind her that it's especially important when she's tired. Frequent mirror checking forces her eyes and mind to work together.

Another sign of fatigue is when your teen has been talking with you and stops. It could be a sign that her mind is drifting and she's losing focus.

Or it could just mean that she's mad at you about something completely unrelated.

When Equipment Fails:
A Master Disaster Plan

Time of sessions: 30 to 60 minutes
Locations: Various

Is fuel efficiency really what we need most desperately?
I say that what we really need is a car that can
be shot when it breaks down.

RUSSELL BAKER

One hot summer, just after I turned 17, several of my cousins piled into an ancient Chevy my parents had bought for us kids to drive. I was showing off in a residential neighborhood, braking hard and taking corners a little too fast. As I approached one corner, I hit the brakes, and nothing happened. The pedal went to the floor. "I don't have any brakes!" I yelled. Everyone laughed, thinking I was kidding.

I wasn't, and the laughing stopped as I jumped a curb, raced across Mrs. Kintner's front lawn, and roared between her house and garage, finally coming to rest in the middle of a garden in her backyard. We were lucky. The rusty brake line had happened to snap at a time and place where we avoided a crash, wounding only pride and a bushel of tomatoes.

Equipment failures happen, always when you least expect it. There are two distinct things your teen needs to know about equipment failures. First, he needs to know what usually happens when a given problem occurs. What does it sound like and feel like in the car? If he has an idea of what's happening, it's less likely he'll panic. Second, he needs to know what to do about it. Each type of equipment failure requires a different response.

He won't know what happens unless you tell him, and he won't remember the proper responses unless you practice them, both verbally and on the road. You can address both issues by using "what if" exercises.

The following won't cover all the causes for mechanical disasters or tell you how to fix them when they happen. Instead, the focus is on getting your teen out of the immediate situation and safely off the road, without making decisions that compound the problem. The goal is to have him understand and be able to verbalize the most important two or three things he should and should not do when the most common mechanical problems happen. If you accomplish that, he'll be more likely to do the right things instinctively when problems occur.

TIRE FAILURE

This is probably the most likely equipment failure your teen will encounter, and it can be hairy. Tell your teen that with a flat tire, he'll normally feel vibration coming from one corner of the car and hear a thumping sound that will go up or down in pitch with the speed of the vehicle. He'll also feel a pull on the steering in the direction of the deflated tire. If it's a blowout, he'll probably hear a sharp bang, then slapping sounds as the rubber disintegrates and bounces off the wheel wells, along with the steering pull and thumping noises.

A front-tire failure will pull the car more quickly in the direction of the damaged tire. Rear-tire failure will cause shaking and vibration as well as steering pull, although the pull will be less sharp than with a front tire. In most cases, he'll be able to maintain a fair amount of control in the event of a tire failure. If your teen experiences a blowout, he should:

- Immediately get off the gas, and get a firm grip on the wheel. Stress that this is another reason he should always keep both hands on the wheel when driving, to be better prepared for mechanical emergencies.
- Steer carefully against the pull of the vehicle, and get a feel for the effect of the tire failure on the car's handling, while losing some speed.
- Brake gently, while checking the lane behind and the surrounding traffic.
- Flip on the emergency flashers, and pull off the roadside, being especially careful of any drop from the road to the shoulder.
- Refer to Chapter 6 for guidance on changing a flat tire.

Loss of Steering

Complete loss of steering control is very rare, but loss of power-assisted steering can occur as a result of number of causes. If your teen inadvertently turns off the ignition switch while driving or if his car has lost enough power-steering fluid, he'll be without power steering. He may receive little in the way of warning other than the steering suddenly feeling stiff. Any time the engine quits—when it runs out of gas or has a major mechanical failure—power steering will be lost, but he'll still retain manual steering. It will feel stiff and require much more effort, but he can still effectively control the car. If your teen loses power steering, he should:

- Get off the gas, and get a firm grip on the wheel.
- Attempt to steer to the shoulder of the road while braking carefully.

If he finds himself in the rare situation of losing all steering control, he should shift to a lower gear and brake very carefully, while praying to come to a stop in a safe place.

BRAKE FAILURE

If your teen's car loses brake-fluid pressure, he'll lose braking power. The brake pedal may lose some resistance to his foot or even suddenly depress to the floor. He could lose all braking or, more likely, just the power-assisted braking. If just the power assist has been lost, there will still be some braking effectiveness if he pushes the pedal hard. If your teen loses any braking response, he should:

- First, pump the brakes to attempt to build back the brake-fluid pressure. This will sometimes bring back some braking power, but he should not attempt to continue to drive if this happens. It's a sign of a problem that needs immediate attention, and he should get the car off the road.
- If pumping the brakes fails to increase braking power, he should shift to a lower gear to help slow down the car.
- Check mirrors, turn on emergency flashers, and pull off to the side of the road when he has slowed down enough to do it safely.

ENGINE QUITTING

A car's engine can shut off when it's out of gas, overheats, or experiences a computer, fuel system, electrical, or other mechanical malfunction or breakdown. Your teen may or may not hear any noise, but he'll feel it in the lack of accelerator response and more difficult steering, since he'll lose the power steering if the engine stops. Have your teen follow this sequence if the motor quits:

- Grip the steering wheel firmly.
- Search for a safe place to pull off the road.
- Brake gently while testing the steering action.
- Check mirrors, and flip on emergency flashers.
- Pull off the road carefully.

GAS-PEDAL PROBLEMS

Accelerator malfunctions can be scary. A broken spring can cause the gas pedal to lie flat on the floor, and he won't be able to bring it back up. He'll also have no control of speed with the pedal. If this happens, he should:

- Brake, and shift to neutral.
- Put on the emergency flashers, and pull off the road.

A stuck accelerator can be even more distressing but is usually fixed quickly. Your teen should:

- Stick his toe under the pedal, and pull it toward him, or kick the side of it. Check to make sure a floor mat isn't jammed against the pedal.
- If this doesn't work, brake carefully, and shift the car into neutral gear.
- Don't turn off the ignition while driving to stop the racing of the engine (he'll lose power steering and power brakes).
- Find a safe spot to pull off and stop, then cut the engine.

Regardless of the type of mechanical failure, if the problem can't be readily fixed, your teen should follow these steps:

1. Call your auto club, preferred towing company, or trusted mechanic (all these numbers should be in the glove compartment), after he notifies you.
2. If the situation is more serious (a dangerous or unfamiliar location, fire, nighttime), call 411 for the nearest police department or 911.
3. Put the hood up and/or attach the white towel or rag from the supplies in your trunk to the antenna or driver's-side door handle to signal the need for help.
4. If within a reasonable, safe walking distance of a restaurant, hotel, or service station with a pay phone, make the calls and await help there.
5. If not, stay inside the car with locked doors while awaiting assistance or towing. Be wary of anyone approaching who offers help or a ride. Decline their offer if help is on the way. Otherwise, use best instincts and judgment. Asking to see identification is not an unreasonable request.

To summarize, in order to prepare your teen for mechanical disasters, talk about the most common types of problems he might encounter, and have him recite back the correct sequence of responses to each one. The first and last correct responses are almost always the same: grip the wheel tightly, and get off the road safely. The responses in between differ. Help him internalize the right sequence with an exercise like this:

"You've just had a tire blowout. How will you know?"

"I'll know because of the sound and the vibration. The direction of the pull of the steering will tell me on which side the blowout occurred."

"Right. So what's the first thing you do, and what do you make sure you *don't* do?"

"The first thing I do is grip the wheel tight and get off the gas. I *don't* want to brake."

"Then what?"

"Then I steer to counteract any pull toward the bad tire, and after I've lost some speed and feel in control, I'll start to brake carefully and slowly."

"Then what?"

"Check the mirrors, make sure I know what's going on with traffic, put on the flashers, and pull off the road slowly and safely. Then call you to fix it."

Take time during Fourth Gear to devote some of your driving time on several different occasions to practice what your teen should do in situations involving mechanical malfunctions. Reinforce those exercises in later driving sessions, by suddenly asking, "OK, what if your brakes failed right now? What would happen, and what would you do?"

Third Gear Accomplishments Checklist

_____ Uses brake lights ahead as an early-warning system, covering the brake quickly as a precaution.

_____ Exhibits proper lane usage on expressways, and consistently checks mirrors and signals before changing lanes.

_____ Is proficient with use of exit and entrance ramps on freeways. Can estimate needed traffic gaps and merge smoothly and safely at highway speed.

_____ Demonstrates proper technique and skill in passing another car on a divided highway.

_____ Demonstrates the unique scanning and visual search skills needed in an urban driving environment.

_____ Understands the five scenarios that cause the most crashes in the city, and knows how to minimize or avoid their risks.

_____ Is confident and competent in turning left across urban traffic, under different right-of-way situations.

_____ Knows the typical mistakes that cause teen drivers to run off the road.

_____ Knows how to avoid running off the road and, if it happens, how to get safely back on the road.

_____ Understands what causes skids and spins and the mistakes most teens make that result in them.

_____ Understands how to avoid getting into a skid or spin and, if it happens, how to recover.

_____ Is aware of and uses some of the techniques professional racers use to stay crashproof, both in handling the car and in attitude.

_____ Recognizes the four basic responses all hazardous driving conditions require.

_____ Can list the primary risks and associated driving strategies for weather-related hazards, including snow, ice, rain, and fog.

_____ Can list the primary risks and associated strategies for dealing with fatigue and driving at night.

_____ Is familiar with the most commonly encountered mechanical disasters, including failures of engine, accelerator, tires, brakes, and steering, and can successfully recite the proper sequence of actions to deal with each.

Fourth Gear:
Reducing Risky Behaviors

During Fourth Gear, the emphasis shifts to behavior, specifically those attitudes and behaviors most dangerous when operating an automobile. The information and exercises in this section arm you with extensive tips and strategies designed to mitigate the potentially negative consequences of distractions, disabling substances, road rage, and speeding.

You'll find fewer step-by-step exercises in Fourth Gear. That's deliberate. You've already worked on most of the fundamental driving skills. Now you're addressing an equally important area: controlling teen impulses that can lead to disasters on the road.

Fourth Gear is where you loosen the reins a little, mixing up the locations and driving times. Have your teen drive for an extended time on a family vacation, a visit to relatives, or a trip into the city, and discuss the attitudes and behaviors discussed in these chapters—your teen's and other drivers'—that can put him or her at risk.

Your teen may have obtained a license by this point, and you can build in solo driving time as he or she shows increasing competence and confidence.

CHAPTER

23

Sharing the Road

Time of sessions: 30–60 minutes
Locations: Various roads and highways

*When I first started learning to drive, I thought the most
important thing was to control my car. Now I know
it's almost as important to watch out for everyone else.
There are a lot of people on the road
who are impatient, incompetent,
or just plain wacko.*

LAUREN SANDERSON, AGE 16

I t's not enough to be a skilled, rule-abiding driver. It's important also
to be able to predict and react to everyone else with whom you're
sharing the road. You can't always tell the incompetents from the lunatics or the merely angry, but different types of vehicles present different kinds of risk, and their drivers give you many clues if you pay
attention. Part of your teen's emerging safety savvy depends on recognizing what to be aware of with each type of highway user and how best
to respond to the challenges they pose.

Get your teen out driving on a freeway or expressway, and talk
through the challenges posed by sharing the road on busy, high-speed
highways.

TRUCKS

Trucks are a little scary for beginning drivers, and rightly so. They will be your teen's constant road companions on freeways and divided highways, so she needs some strategies for dealing with these lumbering beasts.

Professional truckers tend to be better and safer drivers than most people on the road. It's their job; they have lots of experience and daily opportunities to observe the results of driver error. On the other hand, trucks are more dangerous to beginning drivers than most other vehicles.

First, truckers are always in a hurry. They have many incentives to get where they're going as quickly as possible, and their customers expect timely delivery of their goods. So they will often exceed the posted speed limit.

Second, lots of mass carries lots of momentum. Trucks need as much as three times more time and distance to slow down and stop than a car, something not necessarily understood by beginning drivers. And when trucks lock up their brakes, especially on slippery roads, the results are not pretty.

Third, trucks have a higher likelihood of fatigued drivers. Federal regulations limiting the consecutive hours truckers can drive have helped, but they still spend far more time on the highway than other drivers and are more susceptible to highway hypnosis, nodding off, and lapses of attention.

Finally, a truck will win a collision derby every time. Semitrailer trucks can weigh 80,000 pounds, and if you go up against that kind of weight, you're going to lose, and lose big. Large trucks are involved in more than 5,000 traffic fatalities every year, and 98 percent of those fatalities are suffered by passenger-vehicle occupants. That is not the kind of odds you want to mess with.

According to industry statistics, the three most frequent reasons for crashes involving heavy trucks are the following:

1. *The truck's inability to stop in time.* A fully loaded truck can take an incredible amount of time and distance to come to a stop. Avoid truck crashes by giving them far greater following distances, letting them get by you if you are holding them up, and ensuring that you do not brake quickly if a truck is following closely behind you.

2. *A motorist trying to pass a truck on the right while the truck is making a right-hand turn.* Your teen should be aware of how big the right-side blind spot is for a trucker. Not only is there a big blind spot, but trucks also typically require about a lane and a half to get around a right turn. If your teen is behind a truck that signals or starts to turn right, she needs to give it plenty of room to account for these factors.

3. *A motorist riding in the truck's blind spots.* Two key areas need special attention here. First, a car directly behind a truck is usually impossible for a truck to see. As the signs on trucks say, "If you can't see my mirrors, I can't see you." Following directly behind a truck also eliminates your teen's ability to see ahead and puts her in a good position to be pelted with rocks and debris kicked up by the truck's tires. She should stay out of this zone.

   Second, it's difficult for a truck driver to see a car coming up alongside it, especially on the right. In this situation, if your teen can't see the face of the truck driver in the truck's rearview mirror, the driver can't see her. Have her accelerate through a truck's blind spaces as she goes by it, minimizing the time spent in the no-zone.

Other things your teen can do to coexist more safely with trucks:

- In hilly or mountainous terrain, the physics of trucks are amplified. A loaded truck climbing a steep hill may struggle to achieve 35 mph. On the way down, the trucker will risk burning up his brakes to keep his speed under control. Pass trucks on your way up, and stay out of their lane on the way down.
- Trucks need lots of time and room to merge onto highways. Move over, and give them plenty of space to merge into.
- Don't cross lanes directly in front of a truck or sneak into a tiny gap in traffic ahead of a truck. You aren't giving the trucker any margin of error.
- Beware of the effect of trucks on air as you drive past them. Trucks create a vacuum behind and beside them that can pull things toward them. It's significant enough that a bicyclist can draft behind a truck at 60 mph while hardly pedaling. Just outside this area of vacuum, wind turbulence is produced that can rock a car as it passes by.
- Beware of the effect of trucks on water as you drive past them. On rainy days, truck tires throw off waves of water that extend at an angle behind them and can overwhelm a wiper's ability to clear a windshield. Your teen can be blinded for several seconds, with her traction reduced, too. If she is passing or being passed by a truck in heavy rain conditions, have her focus on the road ahead, steering firmly straight ahead until the onslaught subsides.

MOTORCYCLES

Motorcycles present their own unique challenges and dangers.

- Motorcycle drivers tend to be younger, more aggressive, and less safety-conscious. You'll occasionally see them whizzing by on the shoulder or even driving between lanes going 110 mph, without a helmet. They apparently have far more faith in good fortune and other drivers than you should.

- Many middle-agers have taken up motorcycles in the past decade or so, looking for a counterpoint to the sheer joy of driving their minivans. This group has been the primary reason the number of fatally injured motorcyclists has increased by 75 percent since 1997, when those numbers were at an all-time low and the baby-boomer Harley romance began.
- A motorcyclist's rear and peripheral vision is reduced compared with the driver of a car.
- Motorcycles are far harder to see than larger vehicles. Many motorcycle crashes happen because car drivers did not see them well enough.
- Motorcycle operators may not have any training or even valid licenses. In 2003, fully 25 percent of fatally injured motorcycle drivers did not have valid licenses to operate their machines.
- Also in 2003, among motorcycle drivers killed at night, 56 percent had blood-alcohol levels at or above 0.08 percent.

On the other hand, motorcycles can maneuver out of trouble much more quickly than cars. A mediocre motorcycle will crush a six-figure sports car in acceleration and stopping distance. A motorcycle driver tends to have fewer distractions, too. It's extremely difficult to put on eye makeup or conduct a cell-phone call while driving a motorcycle.

Yet motorcyclists are, without doubt, the most vulnerable drivers on the road, much more susceptible to bad weather and poor road conditions and possessing little in the way of physical protection. According to the Insurance Institute for Highway Safety, on a per-mile basis, the number of deaths on motorcycles is about 27 times the number in cars. Motorcycles need plenty of room and respect.

The most important thing for your teen to be aware of with motorcycles is simply to learn to see them. Our eyes get trained to recognize the mass, reflectivity, and dual headlights of cars and trucks. Narrow, silvery motorbikes that can quickly slip into gaps, slide between cars, and show up out of nowhere take many drivers by surprise. They can completely disappear within the boundaries of the right rear blind spots of most sedans, for example.

Cars turning across traffic without seeing motorcycles are a common cause of crashes. When turning left at an intersection after a car passes by, have your teen look through the car's windshield or wait for a second or two after it goes by, to make sure a cyclist is not obscured behind the car. Likewise, when turning right at an intersection or into a driveway, have your teen be careful of motorcycles (and bikes) slipping into the blind spot on her right.

Bicycles

Many teens don't fully understand rights-of-way when it comes to bicyclists. Collisions kill more than 1,000 bicyclists every year. Your teen needs to know that a bicyclist has the same rights (and responsibilities) on the road as the driver of an automobile. Some bicyclists make it confusing by riding on the shoulders of roads and crossing intersections against lights and signs, but they are required to follow the same rules of the road as a driver. They also have every legal right to ride down the middle of an urban street or country road at 15 or 20 mph if they want to (unless there are minimum speeds posted). It may be dangerous, but it's perfectly legal. Your teen should treat bicycle riders much like motorcyclists—with a wide berth and a healthy dose of caution and respect.

OTHER CARS

Cars provide good visibility of their drivers. Your teen should note whether the drivers surrounding her are eating, drinking, minding children, talking on the phone, or otherwise absorbed, perhaps singing a Barry Manilow song. Distracted drivers need more of your teen's attention, as well as an increased following distance.

Your teen has the least amount of control over other drivers, and it's an area where she may underestimate risk. She has little ability to influence another driver's attitude or skill level. The best she can do is to treat every other driver as unpredictable and more likely to make risky decisions than she is. When others drive well, she can be pleasantly surprised and appreciative. When they don't, she won't be surprised, and she'll be prepared for it.

Cars can yield many clues about their drivers. Several types of passenger vehicles can be pegged as more risky than others:

- *The Barker.* Barkers tend to drive late-model luxury sedans and spend every minute behind the wheel with their ears glued to tiny cell phones, making appointments, barking out orders for more widgets, and setting up tee times. To Barkers, focusing on their driving is secondary to maximizing their productivity.
- *The Boomer.* Boomers drive a variety of different types of cars, but each is a traveling concert in a can. With heads bobbing, the car throbbing, and music pounding at ear-splitting decibels, Boomers can't hear, and the music commands attention better spent on the road.
- *The Burner.* These are typically small Japanese models with wings bolted to the rear trunk lid and custom exhaust pipes with six-inch bores, crammed with a minimum of three pim-

ply faced guys. Burners tend to speed, tailgate, and make risky
passes, sometimes at your daughter.

- *The Banger.* Bangers have no sense of protecting their bubble,
  and it's been popped many times. Bumpers hanging, fenders
  dented, red tape on the taillights—these drivers have been
  there, done that, and haven't learned. One dent's a mistake. A
  bunch is a screaming, flashing warning signal.

Have your teen pay close attention to how other drivers express
their skill, attentiveness, and attitude through their choice of car, their
style of driving, and their acceptance of distractions.

Knowing how to share the road safely with all users will help keep
your teen crashproof. As she builds more confidence driving in a variety of situations, have her sharpen her perception and better predict the
actions of her neighbors on the road with the help of the tips outlined
in this chapter. She should be able to recite the major risk factors with
respect to trucks, cars, motorcycles, and bicycles and know how to reduce those risks. She should be able to tell you much about those she
encounters on the road—their challenges, their vulnerabilities, and the
clues they yield about their approach to sharing the road.

CHAPTER 24

Going Fast

*Why is it that everyone driving faster than us is a maniac,
and everyone driving slower than us is an idiot?*

GEORGE CARLIN

One morning, several weeks after moving to Illinois, I was running a little behind on my way to work. I was going about 48 mph in a 35-mph zone and got pulled over for speeding. When the officer came back to the car after checking my Pennsylvania license, he informed me that it was suspended. He pulled me out of the car, put my hands up on the roof, and handcuffed me as my new friends, neighbors, and various strangers passed by, wondering what this perpetrator had done. I was taken to the little town's jail, fingerprinted, and placed in a cell. My protests that my license was not suspended went unheeded. The computer said it was.

The computer was right.

Nearly a year earlier, I had received a speeding ticket in Florida while on a business trip. When I got back home to Pennsylvania, I mailed in the ticket and the fine, but by the time it reached Florida, it was a day late, incurring a five-dollar late fee. Florida eventually notified Pennsylvania of the overdue five dollars, and at some point, Pennsylvania suspended my license because the fee was unpaid. I received no notice of any kind from either state of a fine being overdue or of my license being suspended. In the meantime, I had moved to Illinois. Several weeks after moving, still with my Pennsylvania license, I got the speeding ticket. The policeman's computer showed my out-of-state license suspended, and I went to jail.

It got worse. My wife got me out of jail that day and drove me home, where my in-laws were visiting. It doesn't leave the best impression on your in-laws when you are carted home from jail by their daughter.

When I returned to the police station to get my license back, they said they had sent it to the local courthouse. I went to the courthouse, and they didn't have it. Back to the police station, where they then said they had sent it to the Department of Motor Vehicles in Pennsylvania. The Pennsylvania Department of Motor Vehicles didn't have it, either. Back to the police station, where they said they must have sent it to another local judicial authority. They didn't have it, either. At that point, the police department quit returning my calls.

In the meantime, I couldn't legally drive in Illinois without my Pennsylvania license, and I couldn't get an Illinois license until the whole matter was cleared up.

Two months, a dozen phone calls, a court appearance, and more than $800 later, I finally had taken care of things and ended up with an Illinois license. They never did find my Pennsylvania license. All because of five dollars and a lead foot.

I could rail on about the incompetence of several state motor vehicle departments and the Batavia, Illinois, police department, but this was my fault, and it finally sank into my thick head that it simply wasn't worth gaining a few extra minutes by speeding.

I still occasionally have trouble consistently staying under the speed limit on freeways, but I have been much smarter and slower since that debacle. I've channeled my need for speed into racing, which has had the additional benefit of making me a more skilled driver. More important, the desire to set a better example for my kids made changes in that driving habit necessary, too.

With that mea culpa in mind—and recognizing that the inconvenience and embarrassment of my story are nothing compared with the horrific safety consequences speeding can have—the topic of speeding has to be addressed with your teen. Speeding infractions are far more serious in most states for teen drivers than for adults. Teens have little appreciation for the effect of increasing speed on reaction time, braking, and severity of impact. Speeding has been cited as a major contributing factor in almost one-third of all fatal crashes.

Your teen is almost certain to drive more slowly and carefully while under your supervision than he will when you are not in the car. He wants to please you, impress you, and earn the right to be less conservative away from your watchful eye. So pay attention to hints of things to come. If your teen shows a tendency to speed while driving with you, that tendency will probably be even more pronounced when you're not in the car with him.

Here are nine suggestions to help reduce your teen's probability of speeding:

1. *Don't speed yourself.* Enough said.

2. *Make speeding violations painful.* In most states, this will be accomplished for you, because of comparatively severe penalties for speeding during the first year or two of a teen's driving. Agree to specific consequences for speeding that will have a meaningful impact on your teen in your Crashproof Contract (see Chapter 28).

3. *Help your teen understand the relationship between speed and braking distance.* Braking distance, or the distance it takes for a car to come to a stop under given conditions, does not increase in a linear fashion with speed. There's a serious multiple at work here. Braking distance is a multiple of speed squared. In other words, although 40 mph is only twice the speed of 20 mph, the braking distance needed at 40 mph is four times the braking distance needed at 20 mph. At 60 mph, the speed is

three times that of 20 mph, but the braking distance at 60 mph is nine times (three squared) the braking distance at 20 mph.

Familiarize your teen with this equation: "Increased speed = Decreased time for reaction + Increased distance needed to stop."

4. *Incorporate speedometer checks.* To prevent your teen from increasing his speed without realizing it, get him in the habit of doing a speedometer check every three to four mirror scans. This will also help him develop more consistent accelerator pressure, avoiding that roller-coaster feel of being on and off the accelerator as he tries to maintain a constant speed.

5. *Give him a seriously lucky number: 777.* Give your teen 777 seconds. That's just under 13 minutes, or about the amount of time beyond an appointment when most would consider you to be noticeably late. Help him build in about 777 seconds of lead time ahead of when he's due to be somewhere. A fair amount of speeding isn't for the sheer love of velocity. It's because we're running late. We're overscheduled, and we try to cut it close.

You can affect your teen's "deadline driving." You have influence on his preparation and departure when he leaves the house for school functions, dates, movies, and games. Set the clock ahead in the car by 13 minutes. Exaggerate by 13 minutes the time you tell him you think it'll take him to get to his destination. Help him get ready to be out the door 777 seconds earlier than he might otherwise. If he rushes out the door concerned that he'll be late, he's much more likely to speed, pull into traffic with smaller gaps, and get frustrated and react negatively to things that delay him.

While you're at it, why don't you give yourself 777 seconds, too?

6. *Enlist family members and neighbors.* It's fair game to ask siblings whether they have seen or experienced speeding behavior in your teen. Younger brothers and sisters often love to tattle on their older siblings. Solicit help from neighbors, too. Ask them to let you know if they ever observe your teen speeding. Most will be happy to oblige, as well as grateful when you, in turn, let them know that their teenage son consistently lays rubber on a street just out of sight of their home.

7. *Help him understand the relationship among speed, minutes saved, and his crash risk.* For every 10 mph over 50, the risk of dying in a traffic crash doubles. Ask your teen whether the time saved on a ten-mile trip seems worth the increased risk.

SPEED	TIME TO TRAVEL 10 MILES	TIME SAVED	RISK OF DEATH
50 MPH	12 minutes	—	1x
55 MPH	10 minutes, 54 seconds	1 minute, 6 seconds	1.5x
60 MPH	10 minutes	2 minutes	2x
70 MPH	8 minutes, 34 seconds	3 minutes, 26 seconds	4x
80 MPH	7 minutes, 30 seconds	4 minutes, 30 seconds	8x
85 MPH	7 minutes, 3 seconds	4 minutes, 57 seconds	12x

Courtesy National Safety Council Defensive Driving Course

8. *Install a monitoring device.* Many approaches to monitoring your teen's driving behavior with devices installed in the car are now available, most of them very effective. See Chapter 31 for more information on how to track your teen.

9. *Don't speed yourself.* Did I mention this before?

CHAPTER 25

Road Rage:
Effective Ways to Answer the Anger

Drive like you own the car, not like you own the road.
KRISTIN BACKSTROM, FOUNDER OF SAFE SMART WOMEN

Driving a car can bring out the worst in us. In our shells of steel, we are fairly anonymous and sometimes witness or commit thoughtless acts that we wouldn't ordinarily. We're all human, and we all occasionally make driving errors and misjudgments that annoy or endanger others. These acts trigger mild irritation in some, dangerous anger in others. Getting mad may seem justified, and expressing anger can feel like a healthy form of pressure relief. Your job is to help your teen find other ways to deal with these frustrations without resorting to expressing it behind the wheel.

Teens need to understand that in addition to the inherently stressful activity of driving, a very broad cross-section of adults inhabit the road, all carrying different types of baggage. Some are just waiting for something else to set them off—they've had a bad day at work, had a fight with their spouse or kids, are late for an appointment or otherwise in a hurry. Teens find out quickly about the territorial nature of humans on the road—this is *my* space, *my* lane, *my* right-of-way, *my* path you're blocking.

Combine these factors with drivers under the influence of drugs

208 / CRASHPROOF YOUR KIDS

and alcohol and those without proper training or with impaired vision, hearing, and reflexes, and you've got quite a cast of unknown characters piloting thousands of pounds of steel on the road next to you.

Ask your teen: "Are you going to let other people determine and control your mood?" That's what road rage is. It's people giving up their emotional control to others. Don't let your teen give other drivers that power.

That's easier said than done, of course, but if you don't approach it that way, your teen won't necessarily figure it out. The other lesson is that the same principle works at school, too. I can't tell you how many times my daughter has come home from school miserable. It was almost always because someone did something, or didn't do something, that made her feel put down, inadequate, or disrespected. Her entire evening would be colored by her mood, as would the entire family's relationship with her that evening. A week later, after thinking and talking about it, she could realize that it wasn't worth the emotional energy she gave it.

That doesn't mean she won't come home from school near tears again. It does mean, though, that she has begun to make a connection between what others do and how she allows herself to react to it. The value of hindsight and reflection won't make the next snub from a "friend" any less thoughtless, but she may agonize over it a little less. She is slowly and painfully learning to let others' opinions and actions affect her less deeply. It's the same thing on the road, learning to control the way you let others affect you.

A teen's first task is to understand what typically angers other drivers. Here's a starting checklist, compiled from studies and many people's suggestions. Add your own particular peeves.

10 THINGS GUARANTEED TO ANNOY OTHER DRIVERS

1. Tailgate the car in front of you, following a second or less behind.
2. Pull out in front of someone, and take your time getting up to speed.
3. Fail to use your turn signals when turning or changing lanes.
4. Run yellow or red lights.
5. Show inattention with your driving while gabbing on a cell phone.
6. Park too close to a parking-space line, or, worse, take two spaces.
7. Drive well below or well above the speed limit.
8. Slow way down or stop as you merge onto a highway from an entry ramp.
9. Use your horn to express disapproval or anger, or flip someone a finger.
10. Pass other drivers on the right or on the shoulder.

Even if your teen has not contributed to the irritation of other drivers with any of those behaviors, she will still encounter aggressive and potentially dangerous drivers. The following strategies will reduce the likelihood that she will become a victim of such drivers:

- Get out of their way. If they are speeding, weaving, lane changing, honking, or tailgating, give them your lane, or pull off at a safe place to let them go by. They've already flunked the auto IQ test. It's their problem. Don't make it yours.
- Avoid eye contact. Anthropologists tell us that primates interpret eye contact as threatening. Look straight ahead, and do not lock eyes with baboons.
- If your teen has observed particularly aggressive or dangerous behavior by another driver, she should pull off the road, call

911, and report the offender's license plate number, location, and car type. There's nothing like being questioned by a uniformed officer to alter behavior. She'll feel better, too, getting a little revenge without putting anyone at risk. She'll probably even reduce others' risk by doing this.

Informal surveys have shown that the single most annoying driver behavior is tailgating, so inform your teen that if she tailgates, it will likely have the most negative effect on other drivers. If your teen is being tailgated, her goal is to get the tailgater in front of her. Have her move to the right side of the lane so the tailgater can see oncoming traffic better, then slow down to open a bigger gap ahead for the tailgater to pass her. If the tailgater makes a risky pass into a narrow gap, she should slow down even further to ensure that the pass can be completed.

Until she gets the bumper hugger in front of her, have her signal turns and upcoming slowdowns far earlier than normal, and build additional following distance between her car and the car in front of her.

CULTIVATING CLASSY DRIVERS

A valuable part of what you can instill in your teen is a sense of road etiquette, of highway manners. To teens, *etiquette* sounds stuffy and formal, and *manners* is something they learned as children at the dinner table. So let's call it *class*. Classy people are generally those whose behavior we respect and who respect others. That's exactly the point. Classy drivers understand that all our human foibles—anger, jealousy, inattention, incompetence, impatience—eventually get expressed behind the wheel.

But classy drivers refrain from responding in kind to such foibles. Just as we try to minimize our teens' perception that everyone is paying attention to and making judgments on everything about them—their clothes, their hair, their makeup, their speech—we need to reinforce that when it comes to other drivers, it's not about you! Classy drivers have learned that the road is always shared with an ever-changing parade of unpredictable people and that the experience of driving is much more enjoyable when you don't take their behavior personally.

If we instill in our teens the desire to become classy drivers—worthy of respect—in addition to becoming safer, more competent drivers, it will be easier for them to give the other guy a break, even when the other guy just did something amazingly boneheaded or dangerous.

The important lesson is that your teen can have an impact on those around her, both positive and negative. Keeping her emotions in control and giving out what she'd like to get back will make her driving experience more enjoyable. Classy drivers help create classier driving behavior in others.

Another effective way to reduce road rage is to commit small acts of unexpected grace or kindness. Acts of kindness aren't random, they're very deliberate. It's just that they happen so infrequently that they seem random. It's remarkable how powerful simple courtesies can be in defusing potentially angry encounters. The results can be stunning—in a matter of seconds, you can watch the body language relax, the frown soften, the hand poised to hit the horn return to the wheel. How can you resist something that costs so little and produces so much? Teach your teen to commit deliberate acts of kindness.

10 THINGS GUARANTEED TO MAKE OTHER DRIVERS HAPPY

Below are ten examples of things your teen can do to produce immediate and positive results:

1. Pay the toll of the driver behind you.
2. Give drivers the benefit of the doubt by letting them go first at four-way stops or other "after you" situations.

3. Give them a thumbs-up for no reason. They'll assume you like their car or you think they're hot.

4. Flash them a big smile for no reason. They'll be convinced you think they're hot.

5. Acknowledge your driving errors with an "I'm sorry" look and gesture. We all goof.

6. Give plenty of heads-up time when signaling turns or lane changes.

7. Don't use your cell phone while driving. Pull off the road if you really need to use it.

8. Stay with the flow of traffic, even if it's a little slower or faster than you'd prefer (as long as it's not over the speed limit). You're going to get there at about the same time, anyway.

9. Never, ever hit another parked car's door when opening yours.

10. Sing along with the radio, loudly and with passion. That's always good for a laugh.

When all else fails, she can always quietly recite to herself the SASSY (sane and safe saves you) prayer:

God grant me the serenity
To accept the road conditions I cannot change,
To change the ones I can,
And the wisdom never to get behind this guy again.

CHAPTER 26

Dangerous Distractions

A car is not the only thing that can be recalled by its maker.
UNKNOWN

Jackie Murphy, the mother of two teenage girls, offers a story about teen drivers and passengers that hits very close to home: "When my daughter Brenna was 16, her life changed forever one cold winter night. Brenna's friends Rachel and Tara had been freezing outside the school after a game, waiting for one of their parents to pick them up. They decided instead to ride with Mike and his two friends. Mike had been driving for about three months and had just been presented with a brand-new Lincoln Navigator. His parents thought this would be a safer vehicle for an inexperienced driver. So there were five teens in the truck, and the radio was blasting. Not long after the girls were picked up, Mike went through a stop sign, braked abruptly, spun the car, and smashed into a tree. Rachel wasn't wearing a seat belt and smashed into Tara. The two boys in the front seat were thrown out of the car, and the boy in the backseat broke his leg. The boys were lucky. Tara, an only child, was killed. Rachel cannot walk, talk, or eat on her own and now functions at a fifth-grade level.

"As a result of this accident, we didn't allow either of our daughters to have any passengers for more than six months after she got her license. Both have proven to be responsible drivers. They have slowed down and are very aware of everything on the road, especially other drivers making wrong decisions. All of us wish that those lessons could have been learned without tragedy."

Safe driving requires constant, focused attention. This is not typically a highly developed trait among teens. Helping your teen develop a mind-set of heightened awareness and focus will keep him alive and will keep your car out of the body shop. In earlier chapters, we covered the elements of developing good scanning skills. But focus, awareness, and scanning skills are compromised by distractions and mind-altering substances of various kinds.

The most highly developed driving skills are useless when a driver's mind wanders. A primary goal of the entire learning-to-drive process with your teen is to stress the absolute necessity of constant focus, attention, and awareness behind the wheel. It should actually be physically and mentally tiring for him, especially in the initial stages of learning to drive.

One good way to communicate the inherent risks in driving to your teen is to have him sign up as an organ donor when he gets his license. This simple act clarifies the seriousness of the responsibility of driving, and it might also end up saving a life someday.

Let's look at the most commonly encountered distractions and disabling substances and some of the ways to mitigate these risks.

CELL PHONES AND PAGERS

Cell phones are an exceptionally dangerous distraction while driving. Most require at least one hand to operate, which should be on the wheel. Hands-free phones have not been shown to be any safer, because conversations require focus, which needs to be on the road and other drivers. According to a study by the Harvard Center for Risk Analysis, 2,600 deaths and 330,000 serious injuries in 2001 were caused by cell-phone use while driving.

A team of researchers at Johns Hopkins University conducted imaging tests that showed that our brains can direct resources to either visual or auditory input but have difficulty doing both at the same time (which driving and cell-phone chatting require). David Strayer, a psychology professor at the University of Utah, has published research that concludes that talking on a cell phone while driving creates impairment equal to a blood-alcohol level of 0.08, the threshold for a DUI conviction.

REDUCING THE RISK

This one is simple and straightforward. Don't subject your teen to the risk of cell-phone use in a car. Possessing a cell phone in a car is fine, but under no circumstances should a teen be allowed to answer or make a call while driving. Period. There is no message so urgent that it can't wait a minute for your teen to pull off, park the car, and make the call. Virtually every cell phone now has caller ID and automatic redial. Get soft or flexible on this rule with your teen at his risk.

Consider keeping this rule in place until your teen leaves the nest. He will violate it anyway at some point, but you've kept him safer in the meantime, and some may retain a habit that will make our roads safer and reduce road rage. Few things are as infuriating as an inattentive driver, cell phone glued to his ear, talking with his hands, weaving between the lane markers, and varying his speed by 20 mph.

To give your teen the comfort of having a cell phone in a car for emergencies without the temptation to talk on it, take an old cell phone you've stuck in a drawer, and keep it charged and stashed in the glove compartment. By law, every cell phone in the country (even those disconnected from a current service provider) must have a live 911 capability. As long as there is a signal in the area where the cell phone is and it has power, it can make a call to 911. Remember that unlike with a land-line 911 call, an operator will not be able to track the location of your teen. He will have to tell 911 where he is.

PASSENGERS

Having passengers (especially peers) in your teen's car increases risk phenomenally, a fact many parents are unfortunately unaware of. Research supported by the National Safety Council concluded that each passenger in a new driver's vehicle increases the crash risk by 50 percent. Other studies have shown that cars with two or more teens are four times more likely to crash than those with single drivers. It's agonizing enough when it's just your teen, but the ramifications of crashes involving others are frightening to consider.

Each person added is not only an additional distraction but also an additional influence. One guy saying, "Hey, we might be able to get some air on that bump ahead," is not as forceful as three guys in the backseat chanting, "Air! Air! Air!"

REDUCING THE RISK

During the first six months of supervised driving, no passengers other than the parent should be allowed. Over the next six months to two years, depending on the maturity and trustworthiness of your teen and his friends, gradually allow him to add passengers.

The eye-opening statistics cited above also apply to your teen as a passenger in other teens' cars, too, so his passenger restrictions should mirror your restrictions on his riding with other teen drivers. At least with your teen, you have some sense of how he drives. The odds aren't good that your teen's friends' parents have been as involved as you have in their teens' driving development. (So if you've found this book helpful, recommend it to your friends and neighbors.)

When he does have passengers, the risk is reduced if your teen does not look at them while driving and talking. It's a habit that can be ingrained by example when you are with your teen and you are driving. It's not difficult (or rude) to keep your eyes on the road while talking, so reinforce it with your behavior and your direction to him as he drives and you discuss things together.

Finally, emphasize the designated-driver aspect of carrying passengers. Being a designated driver is well understood and accepted when alcohol is involved, but the concept needs expansion. Your teen has the same responsibility every time he gets behind the wheel—to bring himself and his passengers back safely, with the car undamaged—whether or not he is the sole unimpaired passenger. Make clear to your teen the privilege and seriousness of being responsible for the safety of his friends.

FOOD AND DRINK

Americans love to eat and drink in their cars. A *USA Today* study showed that 17 percent of all food eaten outside the home in this country is eaten in a vehicle. We juggle burgers and ice cream, coffee and Cokes. In most cases, your teen doesn't need to, however. Soon enough, he will be faced with the combination of jobs, commutes, transporting kids, hurried errands, and all the other things that contribute to slurping and munching while driving. Not now, though. Spilled drinks, hot coffee or fries in the lap, fussing with wrappers and packaging—the distractions aren't worth the time saved.

REDUCING THE RISK

If he's hungry or thirsty, stop and take a break. Leave yourself enough time when you're helping your teen learn to drive that you don't feel the need to save a few minutes by dining in the car.

If you also prohibit eating and drinking in your car when your teen drives with friends, your car will be cleaner, too!

RADIO AND CD/STEREO SYSTEMS

Fussing with the radio or CD player is a common distraction and one that has led to a surprising number of fender benders and worse. In addition, big bass is in, and woofer madness has infected many teens, especially boys. Huge subwoofers are a must-have in many teen circles. It's not practical to think that teens will not want to listen to music in the car, so the best you can do is work this distraction in gradually.

REDUCING THE RISK

For the first month, while you are operating in First Gear, don't turn the radio on at all. There are so many new and nerve-wracking things for your teen to learn that he won't complain too much. For the second month, play soothing CDs instead of the radio. You won't have to endure annoying commercials, and he can't change the station. It's almost guaranteed that he won't like your choice of tunes, but the point here is to provide some background music that doesn't require much attention. Besides, it's the parent who could probably use some soothing music at this point.

When you're ready to begin letting your teen listen to the radio in the car, have him preset his favorite stations to eliminate some of the constant station scanning and song seeking that teens are prone to do. Then obtain agreement that if he gets to choose the station, you get to control the volume.

Do your teen a favor, and keep boom boxes out of his car. A major stereo system in his bedroom is one thing. The biggest danger it will pose is to his hearing and your patience. In a car, there's much more at stake. If a teen invests the money it takes to put a monster woofer in a car, he's going to listen to it while driving, right? By allowing superloud stereos in your teen's car, you are saying that you are OK with him driving with jet-engine decibel levels of noise. In addition to the things he won't hear that can be important—sirens, horns, shouts, tires screeching, railroad warning bells, motorcycle engines, and the clunks, buzzes, and pings that can signal car equipment problems—it's impossible to maintain full focus when his mind and body are pulsating to music.

The music isn't the issue. Music adds pleasure to driving, and we all adjust to driving and listening to it. It's the volume that literally will drive him to distraction. If it's important enough to him, he'll get it anyway after he's 18. Be an enabler of focus for him in the meantime.

ANIMALS

Except in rare instances, pets don't belong in cars. It's not a comfortable environment for most pets, and they can be an unpredictable distraction for the driver. They certainly don't belong in a car with someone just learning to drive. If a pet must be transported in a car, make sure that it is in an appropriate carrier, restraint, or pet harness.

Wild animals crossing the road are increasingly common today. Every year, there are more than 500,000 deer-auto collisions, representing 4 percent of all U.S. auto crashes. As suburbia continues its relentless expansion, the natural habitats of dozens of animal species dwindle, increasing the numbers of deer, raccoons, skunks, possums, squirrels, coyotes, and other critters crossing our streets and roads, especially at night.

REDUCING THE RISK

When any animal the size of a deer or smaller crosses the road in front of your teen, he should understand that there is one and only one appropriate response: controlled braking and steering down the middle of the lane. No swerving, dodging, changing lanes, or driving onto the shoulder. It's far better to hit the animal and potentially bang up the car a little than to risk going off the road or colliding with other cars or stationary objects. Sorry, animal lovers, but there isn't a critter (or a piece of sheetmetal) out there that's anywhere close to worth it.

The exception to the above is when the animal is the size of a cow, horse, moose, elk, or bear. In this case, your teen should brake while steering to avoid the animal, because hitting it could be life-threatening to the driver. Even then, it should be a judgment call by the driver based on his escape-route options. An additional consideration: if a driver leaves the road and crashes while avoiding an animal, many insurance companies will classify the incident as driver error. Hitting an animal on the road is considered by most to be an "act of God."

Finally, if you see one animal crossing or on the side of the road, expect others to follow, especially deer.

OTHER DISTRACTIONS

It's absolutely incredible what some people will do while they are piloting an automobile. In addition to all the personal grooming procedures better conducted in the bathroom—ear cleaning, eyebrow plucking, eyelash curling, nail filing, nose picking, mustache trimming, hair curling, and shaving—during a driving career encompassing more than three decades, I've also witnessed drivers do all of the following:

> Change diapers
> Read newspapers
> Urinate
> Kiss
> Punch someone
> Pop a pimple
> Dance
> Write an expense report
> Brush a pet
> Fax a document

Study a blueprint

Change clothes

Watch TV and movies

Program a GPS device

Check e-mail

Text-message

Play video games

Play the harmonica

Breast-feed

Sleep (!)

In addition to the above distractions inside the car, there's plenty going on outside the car. Traffic lights, construction sites, flashing signs, provocative billboards, babes in bikinis, cute guys in jeans, threatening weather, cool cars, attractive scenery—the list goes on and on. It's a wonder there aren't more accidents, when you think about it.

Successful and safe driving is a complex combination of operating a powerful and potentially deadly piece of machinery while deftly dealing with dozens of minor and major distractions. You and your teen have your work cut out for you in cultivating these physical skills and the mental mind-set of constant awareness.

So when you hand the car keys to him, instead of saying, "Be good and be careful," say, "Let's review. No cell-phone use while driving. No additional passengers other than Bobby. Seat belts mandatory. No fast-food garbage left in the car. You'll call me as soon as any of the plans you told me about change. And of course, no smoking, drinking, drugs, or speeding. Now, have a good time!"

CHAPTER 27

Disabling Substances

I killed my three best friends in a car crash because I was drunk.
I will live with the memory of that night, and the pain I have
caused so many people, every day for the rest of my life.
I don't care how you do it, but get this message to your kids: you're
responsible for your passengers, and it's not worth it.
I can't bring my friends back.

SEAN LARIMER, AGE 18

The dangers of mixing alcohol and driving have fortunately received an extraordinary amount of attention in recent years, and much progress has been made in raising awareness and increasing penalties for drivers who drink. Yet it's such an important topic that several summary points need to be made:

- Two out of every five people will be involved in an alcohol-related crash in their lifetime.
- More than 17,400 people died and 800,000 more were injured on U.S. highways in alcohol-related crashes in 2002. The blood-alcohol concentration was greater than 0.08, the legal limit in every state, in 86 percent of these cases.
- Alcohol shortcircuits the brain, giving a false sense of confidence, slowing reflexes, and impairing coordination, focus, and concentration. Any one of these can be dangerous; together, they're potentially lethal.

It's not just alcohol you need to be concerned about, either. A variety of drugs, illegal and legal, that negatively affect driving ability and driver safety are readily available to today's high school students. Consult the Appendix for a chart, compiled by the National Safety Council, that shows the effects of various drugs and intoxicants on your teen and her driving.

Despite these facts and widespread efforts to combat drinking, drugs, and driving, teens will continue to drink and use other intoxicants and drive. You may feel like throwing up your hands, assuming that teens will be teens and there's not much you can do. There *is* much you can do, however. You *can* reduce the odds that your teen will drive intoxicated (or get into a car with someone who is) with the following actions.

EDUCATE YOUR TEEN.

Despite all the antidrinking messages teens get today in a dozen different media, numerous myths still persist among many teens with respect to intoxicants, particularly alcohol. Make sure your teen knows the following facts about alcohol:

- Coffee does not sober up an intoxicated person.
- Strenuous exercise does not, either, nor do cold showers or fresh air.
- Food does not soak up alcohol. Although it may slightly slow the rate of alcohol absorption into your blood, nothing you can do will speed up the biological process of eliminating it from your brain and your bloodstream.
- It takes about an hour for the human body to eliminate one drink's worth of alcohol.
- "Light" beer has fewer calories but the same amount of alcohol as regular beer.

• A bottle of beer, a glass of wine, and a shot of hard liquor all have the same amount of alcohol. You will be impaired at the same rate whether you consume vodka, beer, whiskey, rum, Bailey's Irish Cream, brandy, cabernet, scotch, gin, or tequila.

• Women typically do not process alcohol as well as men, because of their lower weight and more limited production of the breakdown enzyme, alcohol dehydrogenase.

• It takes fewer drinks than most teens think to impair driving or to put them at legal risk. Consider the following approximate figures for a 130-pound and a 160-pound teenager:

130-POUND TEENAGER

DRINKS/HOUR	BLOOD-ALCOHOL LEVEL	SKILLS IMPAIRED
1	.025	Attention Reaction time Visual function
2	.05	Exceeds legal limit for commercial vehicle drivers Attention Reaction time Visual function Emergency response Standing steadiness Eye movement Coordination
3	.072	Attention, reaction time, visual function Emergency response Standing steadiness Eye movement Coordination Information processing Judgment Concentrated attention Speed control
3+	.08	Legal intoxication in all states

160-POUND TEENAGER

DRINKS/HOUR	BLOOD-ALCOHOL LEVEL	SKILLS IMPAIRED
1	.02	Attention Reaction time Visual function
2	.04	*Legal limit for commercial vehicle drivers* Attention, reaction time, visual function Emergency response Standing steadiness Eye movement Coordination
3	.06	Attention, reaction time, visual function Emergency response Standing steadiness Eye movement Coordination Information processing Judgment Concentrated attention Speed control
3+	.08	*Legal intoxication in all states*

And if the above didn't make it painfully clear enough why drinking and driving is such a deadly combination, consider some additional facts.

Alcohol is unpredictable with respect to its effect on your teen's personality and mood. It can make passive kids aggressive or aggressive kids passive, make timid teens violent or turn violent kids into weepy huggers. Happy-go-lucky kids might release repressed anger; quiet, patient kids can become loud and impulsive.

Alcohol affects every motor and perceptive skill critical for safe driving.

Alcohol affects vital visual capacity and functioning.

The problem is, your teen has heard many warnings about alcohol through the years but probably doesn't really know why or how it affects her driving. She knows there's a buzz involved and that it can get her in trouble. But you need to make it more specific; otherwise, your warnings will get lumped into all the other general warnings she's heard, which seem to have such a minor impact on so many kids. So here's the next level of specific information she probably doesn't know.

ALCOHOL AFFECTS THE PHYSICAL AND MENTAL SKILLS THAT KEEP YOUR TEEN CRASHPROOF.

It erodes, blurs, alters, and slows down all of the following:

- The coordination of the eyes, hands, and feet, which lets a driver make the right moves in time to avoid crashes.
- The judgment and reasoning a driver needs to make good decisions to ensure the safety of herself and her friends.
- The attention span needed to stay in control, and a driver needs to be in control every time she drives.
- The memory of all the things you've worked on to help her achieve her driving freedom.
- The response time needed to get out of a dangerous situation.

ALCOHOL MESSES WITH YOUR TEEN'S EYES IN A BIG WAY, INCLUDING:

- *Focus.* It slows the eyes' ability to focus back and forth from objects near and far.
- *Muscle control.* It relaxes the fine muscle control of the eyes, blurring vision.
- *Coordination.* It impairs the eyes' ability to work together, causing double vision.

- *Distance judgment.* It reduces the ability to judge distance accurately.
- *Peripheral vision.* It reduces the ability to perceive things from the side.
- *Night vision.* It limits the eyes' ability to see in low light.
- *Colors.* It impedes the ability to distinguish colors.

And the biggest problem with all these changes? She won't even notice most of them if she's drinking, because her brain is impaired, too.

Finally, emphasize that alcohol is poison to the body. Vomiting is the body's way of ridding itself of a dangerous substance. Have her think about the minimal level of alcohol in her body that puts her at legal risk. Then have her think about the amount that puts her at severe health risk: .3 to .5 of 1 percent of alcohol in her bloodstream, and she's dead.

Many perfectly legal substances can also affect your teen's driving, including prescriptions and common over-the-counter drugs and medications. Review the labels on any prescription drugs your teen uses for allergies, sinus problems, acne, chronic diseases, and other conditions. Some have substances that can stimulate or depress a teen's attention span and alertness. Be particularly wary of medications such as Ritalin and the ever-increasing number of drugs now prescribed to teens to alter moods and combat depression. These drugs are very powerful and lack decades of history and research into all the possible effects they may have on a teen's driving behavior.

Over-the-counter drugs such as antihistamines, cough syrups, and cold medications can cause drowsiness. Remember that your teen is likely to weigh less and potentially be more sensitive than you are to the effects of these medications. A label warning about not operating heavy machinery while taking the medication does not just apply to bulldozers and front-end loaders. If your teen must use an antihistamine, make sure it's a nondrowsy formulation.

SET YOUR OWN EXAMPLE.

Your own responsible use of alcohol and other intoxicants is the single best way to influence how your teen approaches them. If you are out to dinner with your teen, for example, remember that even two drinks can put you over the legal limit for driving and impair your awareness. At parties in your home, it's partly your responsibility to make sure that your guests are fit to drive home when they leave. Serve water or nonalcoholic drinks between alcoholic drinks, and have a plan to help your friends and neighbors who've overindulged get home safely.

Talk with your teen about any prescriptions he is on and whether it could affect his focus or driving ability.

MAKE COSTS AND CONSEQUENCES CLEAR.

Teens also need reminding that in addition to the mental and physical risks associated with their use, the penalties for possession, driving under the influence, and drunk driving have never been so harsh. Loss of license, loss of jobs, stiff fines, court supervision, juvenile homes, sports and school suspensions, jail time—these are serious nightmares, not wrist slaps.

What is less understood is that in many states, if they impair your driving, even perfectly legal drugs can result in some of the same harsh penalties that illegal substances entail, including jail.

Education works best when combined with the specter of costs and consequences, which should be swift and consistent. They should also be painful in a meaningful way to your teen, or it won't influence or change behavior. If she's caught, the state will impose lasting consequences and a damaging addition to her permanent driving record. If you catch her and don't impose costs and consequences, you're an enabler. Consequences you can impose include:

- Restriction or loss of driving privileges and/or license.
- Your teen's assumption of responsibility for increased insurance costs.
- Suspension from school sports teams and other extracurricular activities.

James Bjork is a researcher at the National Institute on Alcohol Abuse and Alcoholism who has been using sophisticated MRI to study brain regions that influence motivation to seek rewards. He's found that teenagers have less activity in these regions than adults, and his results may offer valuable lessons for parents. He advises that when presenting suggestions, anything that parents can do to emphasize immediate payoffs or penalties will be more effective. Using this logic, to persuade a teen to refrain from drinking and driving, you should stress the immediate and the tangible—the fact that if your teen is arrested, you will let her languish in jail for a day or two, for example—rather than simply echoing heard-before warnings about the dangers of driving while under the influence.

KNOW THE COMPANY YOUR TEEN KEEPS.

If you've been paying attention, you know which of your teen's friends you don't trust. While you can't tell your teen what friends to hang out with, you can make it more difficult for her to get together with them or, at a minimum, make it clear that you are uncomfortable with a particular friend and let her know why. You owe her that input. She will reject it to your face, of course. You don't want anyone telling you whom you should associate with, either. But it will register with her nonetheless. Your values are better imparted if they are communicated, and you are well within your rights to express your opinion clearly on this subject.

It's not just the friends you should be concerned with. You should also pay attention to their parents. With some homework and networking, you can find out who the "cool" parents are—the ones who allow teens to drink in their homes. Most of these parents rationalize that they would rather have their kids and other teens drink at home, because at least they know where they are. Among the many troubling aspects of this logic is a very practical one: those kids have to get home. Very few of these parents ensure that there is a designated driver for every kid or call up parents to tell them their teen has been drinking at their house and needs to be picked up. And they are legally liable for every kid, while they are in their home and when they get on the road afterward with a couple of beers in their bellies.

Ask the parents of teens who've been killed or maimed in a crash after one of their parties how "cool" they think those parents are.

Do a postdrive check.

Make sure you have at least a brief conversation with your teen when she comes home. Check her eyes and her speech. Watch the way she moves and walks. If you pay attention, most teens will give you enough clues that their brains have been scrambled a bit that night. A quick good-night kiss can be a very effective alcohol detector. If you detect alcohol on her breath, immediately sit her down, discuss your concern and disappointment, and impose the penalties you've outlined in your Crashproof Contract, discussed in Chapter 28.

Join a local chapter of MADD, or encourage your teen to join SADD.

You may think Mothers Against Drunk Driving (MADD) and Students Against Drunk Driving (SADD) are composed mostly of zealots and teetotalers. In fact, they are made up of people just like you, except that most have experienced firsthand your worst nightmare, and they don't want anyone else to go through what they've gone through. Joining MADD is a great way to reinforce to yourself and your teen the importance of this issue. You'll also gain insight into what has and hasn't worked for others and better understand what it's like to have your life touched, or, more likely, torched, by drinking and driving. More information is available at www.madd.org and www.sadd.org.

INSTALL A MONITORING DEVICE.

See Chapter 31, "Tracking Your Teen."

ORGANIZE A LOCAL DESIGNATED-DRIVER SERVICE.

Mallory Jones, a Gulfport, Mississippi, teenager who started BUSY (Businesses to Save Youth), provides a great example of this approach. After a 19-year-old friend of hers died when he crashed his pickup truck into a tree after an evening at a bar, she decided to make a difference. She started a program, partly funded by local businesses, in which local teens act as designated drivers for fellow students who have been drinking. They have helped deliver hundreds of students safely home.

Critics contend that such an approach tacitly condones teen drinking, and they have a point. On the other hand, local parents and the school system have been supportive, figuring that it's a pragmatic approach to an often intractable problem. Even with a signed Crashproof Contract and their parents' assurances that they want to be called to pick up their teens if they've been drinking, the fact is that some teens will not call their parents. This can be an effective additional alternative, one that your local high school may embrace as both another strategy to reduce teen crash deaths and a worthwhile endeavor for school service clubs to support.

VISIT A REHAB HOSPITAL.

Two types of rehabilitation hospitals can have enormous impact on your teen. Visiting either with your teen takes a little ingenuity and some sensitivity but can usually be accomplished. The first type is a substance-abuse facility, where she can observe the devastating results for people who have rolled the addiction dice and lost. The second type of rehab hospital is one that treats spinal-cord or head injuries, many of which have resulted from a vehicle crash involving alcohol. Most of these hospitals can put you in contact with patients who speak to groups or individuals about their situations, and it can be very powerful.

Call your local rehabilitation hospital, and ask to speak with the administrator or the education department to see if a visit can be arranged or if they have speakers who will share their personal stories.

Bring a small gift or flowers, and thank your lucky stars that your teen is not a patient or a permanent resident.

GIVE HER AN OUT WHEN SHE NEEDS IT.

Talk frankly with your teen about what to do if she is in a situation where she or her friends have been using intoxicants, and she wants to get home safely. Choose a code word for her to use in a phone conversation such as "I've got a lot of homework to do," which means that you will immediately pick her up, with no questions asked or punishment delivered.

This may be hard to do for many teens, but if you give your teen a way to save face with friends in the interest of safety, she may take advantage of it. You've committed to it in the Crashproof Contract, and it's a great way to establish honesty and trust while your teen demonstrates responsible behavior in a difficult peer-pressure situation.

Fourth Gear Accomplishment Checklist

_____ Is familiar with the risks and strategies for successfully sharing the road with trucks, motorcycles, cars, and bicycles.

_____ Can identify potential problem drivers by their behavior, awareness, driving style, and vehicle type.

_____ Understands the relationship between speed and braking distance.

_____ Understands the relationship among speed, minutes saved, and crash risk.

_____ Consistently demonstrates the ability to stay within the speed limit or at a safe speed in all situations and conditions.

_____ Has incorporated, with your help, several strategies to reduce "deadline driving," by building in adequate time to get to destinations.

_____ Is aware of ten or more things that most annoy other drivers and can lead to road rage.

_____ Knows the three key strategies for dealing with an angry driver.

_____ Knows at least ten things to do that will be appreciated by other drivers.

_____ Demonstrates classy behind-the-wheel behavior.

_____ Is aware of the dangers posed by the most common driver distractions, including cell phones, passengers, radio/CD players, food and drink, and others.

_____ Understands how to reduce the risk of each of these distractions.

_____ Complies with any restrictions you've imposed to deal with such distractions.

_____ Understands the dangers posed by intoxicating substances, including alcohol, illegal drugs, and prescription medications.

_____ Is aware of the relationship among the number of drinks, a person's weight, and blood-alcohol concentration.

PART 3

The
Homestretch

You're almost there, and the checkered flag is in sight. Although you may be nearing the end of the most intense part of your involvement, your teen is just beginning what should be a safe and enjoyable lifetime of using one of the most practical and liberating inventions of the past century.

In the remaining chapters, you'll find out about advanced driving schools, where your teen can sharpen his or her skills, reactions, and defensive-driving attitudes even further.

You'll get help choosing a car for your teen, with 75 different models to consider (or avoid) that fit a variety of budgets and crashproof needs.

We'll also take a look at the new ways available to keep track of teens, their cars, and their travels.

Hang on and turn the page. The finish line awaits.

CHAPTER

28

The Crashproof Contract

I hear and I forget. I see and I remember.
I do and I understand.

CONFUCIUS

You've ground through all the gears. You've helped your teen develop driving-related skills and attitudes that will help crashproof him for the rest of his life. The final step? Committing the most important behavioral aspects to writing. All of your behind-the-wheel exercises have laid the groundwork for your teen to improve his driving skills, but the most skilled teen driver is still at high risk if he compromises those skills with risky behavior—cell phones, passengers, speeding, aggressiveness, and intoxicating substances.

Your teen will have to make those choices, and he will be influenced by a series of factors well beyond the scope of this book. You do your part by educating, leading by example, and having constant and ongoing discussions about those choices. The final step is to develop and sign an agreement.

A written agreement may seem too formal to you. You may believe that you have a firm understanding with your teen about these issues. But there is power in the written word, as a symbol of commitment and as a way to express, with little room for misunderstanding, a vitally important pact between you and your teen. The National Institute of Child Health and Human Development released a study in 2005 that showed that when parents of 16-year-olds had their teens review infor-mation about risky driving practices and sign written agreements spelling out consequences, the limits stayed in place for up to a year, and teens reported engaging in less risky driving later on.

A Crashproof Contract sets the expectations, ground rules, and consequences for the use of the car and the behind-the-wheel behavior of your teen. A signed agreement gives your teen very clear guidelines. As with most dealings with teenagers, being very specific can avoid many misunderstandings and circumvent his tendency to act dumb when it's beneficial. A written agreement also forces you to decide up front what your rewards and consequences will be. You don't want to be making up this stuff on the fly, constantly negotiating with your teen, with infractions bartered and traded like pollution credits.

Let's look at some of the issues surrounding the rationale for a Crashproof Contract and examine some ways to make this agreement more effective for you and your teen.

THE CRAVING FOR CONTROL

One of the hallmarks of becoming a teenager is an emerging fascina-tion with control. He's making more decisions about his interests, what he wears and eats, and whom he chooses to hang out with. Yet at the same time, he feels as if he has little control over his daily life. His par-ents try to influence his hair and dress. His school gives him a series of rules and regulations governing his conduct, his dress, and the classes he needs to take. He must rely on someone else for money, transporta-tion, and a host of other necessities, and his parents try to have some in-fluence on every aspect of his life. Teens crave control, wherever and whenever they can get it.

You can put this craving to good use when discussing auto-related risks with your teen. The fact is, every time he makes a risky decision—speeding, drinking, driving while fatigued, carrying rowdy passengers—he gives up a huge element of his control of the situation. Loss of this control leads to crashes, which lead to even greater loss of control, privilege, and trust.

Make clear to your teen that the responsible use of an automobile is a crucial part of his passage toward adulthood and more control of his own life. Driving a car is a test of maturity, and the real test is when he is beyond your watchful eyes. If he can handle all the demands and temptations that come with operating a car, it's a significant step. The freedom and trust he seeks have to be earned, and they have to be earned in increments. Betraying or abusing that trust is a clear sign that he's not yet ready for the responsibility.

Earning your trust leads to his gaining increased responsibility and freedom—in other words, control. Appeal to his natural hunger for control by insisting that he make good driving decisions. Crashproofing is an active, ongoing process that he has ultimate control over. You've simply jumpstarted what should be a lifelong discipline.

THE IMPORTANCE OF CONSEQUENCES

Motivating your teen to make good choices while driving is just as hard as motivating him to do any of the other difficult stuff that is part of growing up. You can scare, cajole, plead with, threaten, bribe, reward, and educate him. I recommend a healthy mix of all of these, but two will yield the most benefit: the potential loss of parental trust and the certainty of meaningful consequences.

Dr. Peter Sheras, an expert in adolescent development, notes the following in his book, *I Can't Believe You Went through My Stuff!*

I ask teens, "What do you hate most that your parents say to you, what really hurts?" Invariably, they tell me, "It's when they say, 'I'm so disappointed in you.' Or 'I just can't trust you again.' "

He does want you to see him as worthwhile, as worthy of your trust. In fact, it's a fine idea to articulate this in so many words, to say, "I don't want to lay down these rules and limits and consequences, but I'm going to do it because it needs to be done and because you're worth it."

Disappointing parents and losing their trust affect many teens more than temporary loss of privileges, grounding, or scolding. If you need to make a lasting impression with your teen, let him know he's disappointed you or temporarily lost some trust he'll have to work to regain. That alone is painful punishment for most and can often trigger more effort at changing behavior than restrictions or take-aways.

Meaningful consequences also have lasting effects on behavior. You'll need to establish consequences for poor choices and risky behavior, as well as rewards for good choices and responsible behavior. Although the severity of the consequences should fit the behavior, it's even more important that consequences are swift and consistent, or they'll quickly become empty threats.

Remind yourself that his brain is still developing, even as ours atrophy. You hope he remembers the skills and the statistics and the attitudes, but you know he'll remember the penalties and the prospect of privileges lost. It's human nature. We're acutely sensitive to avoiding pain, and its potential presence has a powerful effect on our behavior.

When you clearly outline the terms of car usage as well as the penalties for violating them, punishment can be very straightforward. Dr. Anthony E. Wolf, a clinical psychologist and author of the book *Get Out of My Life—But First Could You Drive Me and Cheryl to the Mall?* suggests that every time a teen breaks a rule or an agreement, there should be a confrontation. He describes three parts of such a confrontation:

1. A clear statement that the rule has been broken.
2. Emphasis that such behavior is not acceptable.
3. A declaration that the rule remains in effect.

The beauty of this approach is that it does not attempt to argue the circumstances of the violation or negotiate an outcome. It simply restates what was already agreed upon and lets the teen know that violations have rapid and predictable consequences.

Positive and negative incentives can be established around many things, including:

- The amount of time before you give approval to obtain a learner's permit.
- The amount of time before you give approval to obtain a license.
- The funds you both will contribute to gas, insurance, maintenance, and other costs.
- The hours of the day or night during which he is allowed to drive.
- The number of miles or hours per week he can drive.
- The locations he can drive to and from.
- The number of passengers who can be in the car when he drives.

If you don't specify the penalties, you'll have to decide on them each and every time there's an infraction. I've left it open in the sample contract but suggest that you set specific penalties. For instance:

VIOLATION	PENALTY
Failure to use seat belts	Forfeit driving privileges for ___ (days) (weeks)
Multiple passengers while driving	Forfeit driving privileges for ___ (days) (weeks)
Speeding ticket	Forfeit driving privileges for ___ (weeks) (months)
Riding in a car where alcohol or drugs were used	Forfeit driving privileges for ___ (weeks) (months)
Being responsible for a crash	Forfeit driving privileges for ___ (months) (years)
Use of alcohol or drugs	Forfeit driving privileges for ___ (months) (years)

Decide on the terms of your Crashproof Contract with your teen's input before he drives without supervision. If he protests that none of his friends has to sign such an agreement, after the obligatory explanation that his friends are not your children, do his friends and his friends' parents a favor, and negate that argument at the same time. Give his friends' parents a copy of the Crashproof Contract. Even if they don't decide to use it, those parents should appreciate the thought, and you may gain some consistency in terms of what's acceptable when the teens drive together. If several of your teen's friends have similar deals, he won't feel singled out, and he'll have one more thing to commiserate about concerning his unreasonable parents.

Putting your names on that piece of paper adds a final touch, the culmination of your journey together. Don't let your teen drive independently until you have worked out an acceptable agreement. The following sample Crashproof Contract is a start. It is also available for downloading and customization at www.crashproofyourkids.com.

THE CRASHPROOF CONTRACT

This agreement reflects our joint expectations, promises, and responsibilities with respect to driving and use of a car. We enter this agreement in good faith, having considered these points to be fair, reasonable, and in both of our best interests.

TEENAGER

I agree that learning to drive, obtaining my license, and operating an automobile are hard-earned privileges, not rights. I will treat these privileges with respect, knowing that demonstrating skill, maturity, and good judgment can expand them, and lack of such will lead to restriction or withdrawal of these privileges.

I realize that every time I get behind the wheel, I am responsible for my safety and well-being, as well as the safety and well-being of anyone else riding with me. I take this responsibility seriously and will not knowingly endanger myself or passengers who have entrusted their lives to me.

I will not let anyone else drive a car I am entrusted with, without the explicit consent of my parents and the other driver's parents.

Seat belts are mandatory not only for me but for everyone else who is a passenger in the car. Every time. No exceptions.

I understand that for every passenger in my car, I increase the likelihood of a crash by 50 percent, and I accept full responsibility for the safety of my passengers when I drive. No passengers will ride with me unless I have explicit consent from my parents.

I will not answer or make a cell-phone call while I am driving. I agree that no call is so urgent that I can't pull over and make it when I am off the road.

I agree not to drink any alcohol or take any illegal or mind-altering substances and attempt to drive. I will not get into a car driven by anyone who I know or suspect has been drinking or taking drugs. If I find myself in this situation, I will call my parents for a ride, with no questions asked.

I agree to keep my speed at or below the posted speed limit at all times and to obey all traffic regulations and laws.

I agree to drive with courtesy for everyone else on the road. When other drivers make stupid moves, I understand that it is not about me, and I will not take it personally or show my irritation.

I understand that violation of any of the above may result in the withdrawal, restriction, or complete loss of any driving privileges my parents see fit, for a duration they determine.

PARENT

I am committed to helping you become the safest, most skilled driver possible and will spend as much time with you as necessary to accomplish this.

When you are driving, I will try my best to limit criticism and shouting. I pledge to be patient while you learn.

I acknowledge that I am not a perfect driver, but I have years of accumulated experience and wisdom to share, and no one in the world cares more about you. I will strive to improve my bad driving habits as I try to teach you good ones, and when in doubt, do as I say, not as I do.

If you have been drinking or are otherwise impaired or if someone driving a car you are a passenger in is impaired and you call me to take you home, I will consider that to be a responsible act, and I will pick you up without lectures or penalties.

It is my responsibility, and I take it seriously, to reduce, restrict, or withdraw any of your driving privileges if I believe it is in your best interest. I don't expect or need you to agree with or like those decisions. I don't like to make them, either. It's totally up to you to avoid them.

It will also be my pleasure to grant, expand, or accelerate your driving privileges as you earn them, and I will be proud to do so.

_____   _____

Teen's signature   *Date*

_____   _____

Parent's signature   *Date*

CHAPTER 29

Advanced Driving Schools
and Programs

The one thing that unites all human beings, regardless of age,
gender, religion, economic status or ethnic background,
is that, deep down inside, we ALL believe that we are
above-average drivers.

DAVE BARRY

Should you consider an advanced driving school for your teen?

Proponents argue that these programs are unique in allowing teens to experience the limits of performance and car handling in a controlled, safe environment. Many catastrophic crashes start with a loss of traction or control, with subsequent driver actions that worsen and compound the problem. Supporters point out that you can't know how different responses affect the losing and regaining of control and traction unless you have experienced them.

Detractors assert that the benefits of such training are typically short-lived and that safe, alert, and sober drivers will very seldom end up needing to recover from a skid or a spin. If you are aware and on top of things, evasive maneuvers are not as necessary, and speedy reaction times are not as critical. Drivers should work on behavior and attitudes, they would emphasize, rather than the skills needed in situations that can be avoided by sensible, in-control driving.

Although there have been some contradictory results, most studies have concluded that graduates of advanced driving schools do not have substantially lower crash rates. Some studies, in fact, indicate that drivers who have been through these programs actually have higher crash rates, perhaps because of an increased tolerance for risk or a falsely elevated sense of skill in emergency situations.

Some school operators dispute these data with their own, showing reduced crash rates for their graduates, and others have begun providing data to traffic agencies and research centers to add validity to their approach. Because so many different factors and measuring techniques are involved, it's difficult to nail down definitive statistics regarding driving-school graduates and crash rates.

So why consider an advanced driving school? Because stuff happens. Specialized training has the potential to give your child an edge and increase the odds that she will respond better in some hazardous situations she may encounter on the road. With professional supervision and custom simulated conditions, advanced driving schools can be good places to develop additional skills, which, among others, can include higher-speed steering, stopping, and skid control.

You must, however, consider the mind-set of your teen and make wise choices in deciding who is suitable for such a course. Advanced training can be helpful for a teen who is a timid driver, one who would never purposely test the limits of traction and control in a car. It can be an invaluable confidence builder for a teen to know how to brake in an emergency, correct a skid, avoid a spin, and better understand the interaction of tires, traction, and steering response.

On the other hand, if you have a confident, aggressive teen driver, be cautious when considering such a program. If you have a son with more than his fair share of testosterone, for example, who has shown an interest in and inclination for speed and thrills—video games, minibikes, street-racing friends—an advanced driving school can potentially encourage riskier behavior. Your teen may feel even more invulnerable and skilled than usual because he's had additional training.

If you do want your teen to attend such a school, I suggest that you enroll her only after she has had at least two years of spotless driving under her belt. She will be much better equipped to appreciate and take advantage of the concepts than a raw 16-year-old driver.

With all of the above noted, an important distinction needs to be made with respect to programs billed as advanced driving schools in this country. Virtually all are, at their core, racing schools that have added teen-oriented programs focusing on the trio of skid control, high-speed steering, and emergency braking.

Advanced driving schools in other countries, notably Great Britain, have long offered extensive curriculums devoted to more sophisticated development of driving skills and behavior, but there are very few like them in the United States. I can recommend one, however, that can accurately be called an advanced driving school, with founders and instructors who have impeccable credentials:

Advanced Drivers of America. Based in western New York, with a regional office in San Jose, California, ADA offers courses in various locations throughout the United States and Canada. ADA teaches what knowledgeable safety experts consider to be one of the best methods of advanced driving, based on the Roadcraft "System of Car Control," as developed since 1935 by the British Traffic Police. Their programs specifically avoid racetrack techniques and emergency evasion tactics. For more information, check out ada@driveandstayalive.com, or call 716-632-5502.

Following is a sampling of some of the better-known and more highly regarded racing schools around the country, most of which offer programs lasting from four hours to two days, costing from $350 to $900 per day. Check their Web sites for current classes and prices, and be aware that some schools may also offer periodic programs at locations other than their listed headquarters.

- *Advanced Driving Dynamics.* Irwindale Speedway, Irwindale, California. One-day courses cover braking technique, skid control, and responses to emergency road situations. www.advanceddrivingdynamics.com or 714-974-4233.
- *Audi Driving Experience.* Road Atlanta Raceway, Braselton, Georgia; Sebring International Raceway, Sebring, Florida; Texas International Speedway, Fort Worth, Texas. Run by the well-known Panoz Performance Driving School, this school offers one- and two-day teen driving schools, covering a variety of car-control and defensive-driving techniques. www.audidrivingexperience.com or 888-282-4872.
- *Bob Bondurant School of High Performance Driving.* Chandler, Arizona. One- and two-day packages teach skid control, braking, cornering techniques, and crash avoidance. www.bondurant.com or 800-842-7223.
- *BMW Teen Driving School.* BMW Performance Center, Spartanburg, South Carolina. Advanced crash avoidance and vehicle control techniques, as well as driving basics, are taught in one- or two-day courses. www.bmw.usa.com or 888-345-4269. Also check your local chapter of the BMW Car Club; some sponsor one-day Street Survival Teen Driving Schools (www.streetsurvival.org), where teens can practice emergency maneuvers on a closed course.
- *Bridgestone Winter Driving School.* Steamboat Springs, Colorado. America's only winter driving school offers Cruise Control, a teen driving program, and teaches specialized driving techniques appropriate for winter and other hazardous driving conditions. www.winterdrive.com or 800-WHY-SKID.
- *Driver's Edge.* Las Vegas, Nevada. Former professional racer Jeff Payne offers free half-day courses for 15-to-20-year-old drivers in braking, skid control, lane changing, and emergency driving

situations. Check www.driversedge.org for classes and locations around the country, or call 877-633-EDGE.

- *ESPN Russell Racing School.* Infineon Raceway, Sonoma, California. Advanced racing instruction is offered, as well as a half-day Highway Survival Course, which teaches car control and accident-avoidance techniques such as threshold braking, skid control, and high-speed handling. www.racingschools.com or 877-463-7223.

- *Fast Lane Teen Scene Defensive Driving Course.* Willow Springs Racetrack, Los Angeles, California. This one-day teen program covers car handling and crash-avoidance maneuvers. www.raceschool.com or 888-948-4888.

- *Mid-Ohio School.* Mid-Ohio Sports Car Course, Lexington, Ohio. The one-day Honda Teen Defensive Driving Program teaches braking, lane change, and skid- and crash-avoidance techniques. www.midohio.com or 877-793-8667.

- *New Driver Car Control Clinic.* Various locations. Half-day seminars place teen and parent in a car while experts communicate instructions about braking and crash-avoidance maneuvers. www.teendrivers.com or 800-862-3271.

- *Skip Barber Driving School.* Mazda Raceway Laguna Seca, Monterey, California; Sebring International Raceway, Sebring, Florida; Road America, Elkhart Lake, Wisconsin; Lime Rock Park, Lime Rock, Connecticut; Daytona International Raceway, Daytona, Florida. Each Skip Barber location offers one-day new-driver programs, covering braking, skid control, lane changing, and road etiquette. www.skipbarber.com or 800-221-1131.

CHAPTER 30

Selecting a Vehicle

Never buy your teen the car you wish you had as a teen.
That's what middle age is for.

THE AUTHOR

The reasons for 15-to-18-year-olds not to own a car far outweigh those in favor, but if you want your teen to have her own car, how do you sort through all the information and choose the best one? That subject merits coverage well beyond this chapter, but your choices can be narrowed considerably if crashproofing is a major priority. The usual evaluation criteria of price, reliability, resale value, performance, style, and safety still apply, but their order of priority changes.

You already know that your teen is far more likely to be involved in a crash and will be much more expensive to insure than older drivers. For many parents, that rules out brand-new cars.

Many teens, boys in particular, are more likely to speed yet are inexperienced in driving difficult-to-handle or high-performance vehicles, so sports cars, heavy pickups, and big SUVs can be disasters waiting to happen.

If your teen does get in a crash, you want to maximize the odds that she will not be seriously injured, which makes crashworthiness and safety features more important and rules out most subcompact cars.

With all these factors in mind, the best car for your teen might:

- Cost less than $5,000.
- Have some basic safety features such as air bags and antilock brakes.
- Provide enough power for decent performance but not enough to abuse.
- Be mid-size or larger, with enough mass to add additional protection.
- Offer high visibility.

In other words, a 1997 fire-engine-green Chevy Lumina.

If that model is not available or acceptable, once you've determined a budget for your car purchase, consider the following characteristics that have the most impact on safety:

FEATURES THAT HELP AVOID CRASHES

Antilock brakes, when used correctly, provide valuable control in emergency braking situations. Vehicles equipped with all-wheel drive can help drivers maintain traction and control in slippery driving situations.

Electronic stability control (ESC) systems sense throttle, steering, and brake inputs and help with directional control by automatically applying the brakes to one or more of the wheels, aiding vehicles that might otherwise lose control or run off the road. ESC systems may prove to be the single most important crashproof safety feature developed in several decades, because research indicates they can actually prevent crashes. A Japanese study revealed that ESC reduced single-vehicle crashes by an astounding 35 percent and head-on crashes by 30 percent. A European study reported that in cars with ESC, crashes of all kinds dropped 16 percent, and single-vehicle crashes fell 29 percent. Especially if you buy a larger vehicle with a high center of gravity such as a sport-utility vehicle, get it with ESC. Of all the extras and add-ons and upgrades you can purchase, this is the most important one for safety.

Daytime running lights have proven to reduce crashes substantially. If the car you're considering doesn't have them as standard equipment, you can get similar results by keeping the headlights on at all times.

Silver may be safer. A New Zealand study cited in the *Berkeley Wellness Letter* found that occupants of silver cars had nearly half the risk of serious injury compared with red, blue, white, and yellow cars, after considering other factors. Black and brown cars were found to be four times as risky as silver. (Other research has suggested that this is because silver is a preferred color among the middle-aged, a group already less likely to have crashes.)

ROLLOVER POTENTIAL

Crashes involving vehicle rollovers have higher fatality rates than other types of crashes and cause more than 10,000 deaths a year. Almost all rollovers happen when a car runs off the road and either strikes an object or otherwise experiences a sudden imbalance in the wheels, flipping the car. Vehicles that are more top-heavy and have a higher center of gravity (SUVs, pickup trucks, and vans) roll over more easily under the same circumstances than passenger cars. Recent studies have shown that SUVs are three times more likely to roll over in single-vehicle crashes than regular cars.

It should be noted that some of these types of vehicles can provide advantages in hazardous weather conditions and add a significant margin of safety simply by virtue of their overall weight. Remember that although four-wheel drive will normally provide better traction in slippery conditions, it won't necessarily provide shorter stopping distances. SUVs, on average, need more distance to stop even on dry pavement than mid-sized passenger cars, because they weigh more and their momentum carries them farther.

Teens who are unlikely to speed or take corners too fast and who know how to deal safely with a car leaving the road may be as safe in an SUV as in a passenger car, but if you have any doubts whatsoever about those factors, definitely avoid these types of vehicles for your teen.

FEATURES THAT PROTECT OCCUPANTS

AS A GENERAL RULE, BIGGER IS BETTER.

A very direct and consistent correlation exists between vehicle weight and the incidence of serious driver and passenger injury, as a result of basic physics. When a 375-pound lineman runs into a 180-pound tailback, there's little doubt who's going to end up on the ground. In head-on crashes, the presence of a driver air bag reduces the likelihood of the driver being fatally injured by 27 percent, but the same driver-fatality reduction is also gained simply by adding an additional 297 pounds of vehicle mass. The death rate in smaller, lighter cars is double that in large cars. The lowest death rate of all is for minivans. (That may have more to do with minivan drivers tending to be parents hauling kids and other precious cargo, however.) Better car design and materials will eventually reduce the advantage weight confers, but for the foreseeable future, bigger is still better.

STRUCTURAL DESIGN SOFTENS THE BLOW.

Most newer cars have sophisticated frames designed with crumple zones, steel reinforcements, and impact-absorptive materials, providing much better crash protection than many older cars. Stick with vehicles that have achieved four- or five-star crash-test ratings for both front- and side-impact tests from the National Highway Traffic Safety Administration (NHTSA) and/or a "good" rating from the Insurance Institute for Highway Safety (IIHS).

DRIVER FATALITIES PER BILLION VEHICLE MILES

VERY SMALL FOUR-DOOR CARS	11.56
SMALL FOUR-DOOR CARS	7.85
COMPACT PICKUPS	6.82
MIDSIZE FOUR-DOOR SUVS	6.73
SMALL FOUR-DOOR SUVS	5.68
MIDSIZE FOUR-DOOR CARS	5.26
LARGE PICKUPS	4.07
LARGE FOUR-DOOR SUVS	3.79
LARGE FOUR-DOOR CARS	3.30
MINIVANS	2.76

Courtesy National Safety Council Defensive Driving Course

IF YOU CAN'T OUTWEIGH THEM, OUTCUSHION THEM.

Air bags, always in conjunction with seat and shoulder harnesses, can make a huge difference in reducing injuries. The more and the newer, the better. Air bags used with lap-shoulder belts reduce fatality risk by 50 percent. Side-impact air bags provide valuable additional insurance in areas with limited structural protection, and curtain air bags give crucial protection to the head in side-impact and rollover crashes.

IF YOU CRASH, GET SOMEONE THERE FAST.

A significant factor contributing to increased fatality rates seen in rural areas is the extra time it takes for emergency help to arrive in crashes. On-board Global Positioning Systems (GPS) such as OnStar can immediately notify emergency personnel of a car's location and summon assistance.

SUGGESTED AUTOMOBILES

Echoing many of the above considerations, in a March 2, 2005, feature on teen driving, *USA Today* pegged key considerations for teen cars to include the following:

- Four- or five-star rating from NHTSA on both front and side crash tests.
- Four- or five-star NHSTA rollover rating.
- Weight of at least 3,300 pounds.
- Acceleration from 0 to 60 mph in 8 to 11 seconds.
- Antilock brakes and side air bags.

The cars *USA Today* suggested, in various classes, all of which meet the above criteria:

SEDANS

Buick LeSabre, 1997–2005
Chevrolet Impala, 2000–2005
Ford Crown Victoria, 2004–2005
Ford 500, 2005
Honda Accord, 2001–2005 (four-door, four-cylinder)
Infiniti I30, 1998–2001
Lexus ES300, 1998–2003
Lexus ES330, 2004–2005
Lincoln LS, 2001–2005 (V-6)
Mercedes-Benz C240, 2003–2005
Mercury Grand Marquis, 2003–2005
Mercury Montego, 2005

SUVS AND WAGONS

Chrysler Pacifica, 2004–2005
Subaru Forester, 2004–2005
Subaru Outback and Legacy, 2000–2004
Toyota Highlander, 2004–2005
Volvo XC90, 2003–2005

MINIVANS

Chevrolet Venture, 2004–2005
Chrysler Town & Country, 2004–2005
Dodge Caravan and Grand Caravan, 2004–2005
Ford Freestar, 2004–2005
Ford Windstar, 2001–2003
Honda Odyssey, 2000–2004
Mercury Monterey, 2004–2005
Nissan Quest, 2001–2005
Toyota Sienna, 2001–2005

The following ten cars were noted by *Kiplinger's* magazine in September 2004 as representing a combination of virtues, including good reliability, decent safety features, reasonable insurance costs, and top crash-test scores. Three-to-five-year-old models of each can be picked up for about $7,000 to $14,000:

2002 Buick LeSabre Custom
2002 Ford Taurus SE
2003 Honda Accord DX
2004 Mazda 6i
2000 Nissan Altima GLE
2003 Saturn Ion Level 1

2003 Subaru Forester 2.5X
2004 Toyota Corolla CE
2003 Volkswagen Golf GL
2003 Volkswagen Passat GL

How about good value per pound? According to 2005 data from Edmunds.com, these five cars have adequate mass and experience steep depreciation in the first year or two, and each can be purchased slightly used at an average discount from list price of about 30 percent:

Buick Park Avenue
Chevy Malibu
Dodge Stratus
Ford Taurus
Mercury Sable

Want a vehicle that fares well in terms of fatality rates? The Insurance Institute for Highway Safety, based on data collected from 2000 to 2003 on 1999 to 2002 models, found that the average model had 87 fatalities per million registered vehicles. These data can't account for all the differences in drivers and their machines, of course, but these vehicles fared far better (first list) and far worse (second list) than the norm:

HIGHEST FATALITY RATE PER MILLION REGISTERED VEHICLES

CHEVROLET BLAZER, TWO-DOOR	308
MITSUBISHI MIRAGE	209
PONTIAC FIREBIRD	205
KIA RIO	200
KIA SPORTAGE, FOUR-DOOR 2WD	197
CHEVROLET BLAZER, FOUR-DOOR	190
FORD EXPLORER, TWO-DOOR	187
CHEVROLET CAMARO	186
MAZDA B-SERIES	185
CHEVROLET TRACKER	183
CHEVROLET S10	182
CHEVROLET CAVALIER, TWO-DOOR	168
CHEVROLET CAVALIER, FOUR-DOOR	162
KIA SPORTAGE, FOUR-DOOR 4WD	162

LOWEST FATALITY RATE PER MILLION REGISTERED VEHICLES

MERCEDES E-CLASS	10	MERCEDES S-CLASS	25
TOYOTA 4RUNNER	12	NISSAN PATHFINDER	25
VOLKSWAGEN PASSAT	16	CADILLAC DEVILLE	26
LEXUS RX300	17	NISSAN QUEST	26
TOYOTA RAV4	18	TOYOTA CAMRY SOLARA	27
HONDA ODYSSEY	19	CADILLAC ELDORADO	29
MERCURY VILLAGER	21		

Longing after an SUV but concerned about their rollover tendencies? In 2004, NHTSA ranked the best and worst, rating the chance of rollover in a single-vehicle crash and determining whether vehicles tipped onto two wheels in a newly designed driving test:

TOP 10 SUVS

MAKE	MODEL	CHANCE OF ROLLOVER	TIP?
CHRYSLER	Pacifica 4x4	13.0%	No
CHRYSLER	Pacifica 4x2	14.0	No
NISSAN	Murano 4x4	15.1	No
HONDA	Pilot 4x4	15.9	No
NISSAN	Murano 4x2	15.9	No
VOLVO	XC90 4x4	17.9	No
BUICK	Rainier 4x4	19.1	No
CHEVROLET	TrailBlazer 4x4	19.1	No
DODGE	Durango 4x4	19.1	No
GMC	Envoy 4x4	19.1	No

BOTTOM 10 SUVS			
MAKE	**MODEL**	**CHANCE OF ROLLOVER**	**TIP?**
MERCURY	Mariner 4x2	23.7%	Yes
JEEP	Liberty 4x2	24.6	No
CHEVROLET	Tahoe 4x4	26.3	Yes
GMC	Yukon 4x4	26.3	Yes
FORD	Explorer 4x4	27.9	No
CHEVROLET	Tahoe 4x2	28.3	Yes
FORD	Explorer 4x2	28.3	Yes
GMC	Yukon 4x2	28.3	Yes
MERCURY	Mountaineer 4x2	28.3	Yes
FORD	Explorer 4x2	34.8	Yes

Finally, the higher-end European cars—Mercedes-Benz, BMW, Audi, and particularly Volvo—have long made safety a high priority in their manufacturing. Used models with relatively high mileage can provide excellent safety and performance at more reasonable prices. For the most recent car recommendations for teens, check *www.crashproofyourkids .com.*

SPENDING INSURANCE MONEY WISELY

After you've bought the car, you get to experience the shock and dismay of insuring it. Here's how to spend that money most effectively:

- Add your teen to your policy rather than buying separate coverage. The rates will typically reflect a combined history of all drivers on the policy.

- Unless your teen drives an insured vehicle more than anyone else, you will save additional money by designating her as an occasional driver rather than a principal driver.
- Insurance costs will be far higher on new and sporty cars and higher on two-door cars than on four-door cars.
- If the car is more than six or seven years old, consider buying liability insurance but not collision or comprehensive insurance, or at a minimum, get a high collision deductible.
- Get plenty of liability coverage, at least 100/300/50.
- If you don't already have one, get an umbrella policy that adds at least $1 million to your auto or homeowner's liability protection. It's comparatively cheap insurance, and it's frighteningly easy to run up seven-figure medical and legal costs with catastrophic crashes.
- Recheck your rates frequently. Many rates for teens drop every six months to a year.
- Some insurers will give a discount if your child has a B average in school.
- Have your teen be responsible for paying an affordable portion of her insurance costs. Determine from your agent exactly what the increased amount would be if she gets a traffic violation, and let her know that she will be responsible for the entire amount of any such increase.
- Some insurers offer discounts if teens answer surveys about their driving attitudes and fill out a log sheet recording details of a specified number of driving episodes shortly after they are licensed. Understanding this, you may be able to talk your agent into an additional discount by pointing out that you are following the Crashproof Plan, have signed a Crashproof Contract, and will spend many hours of supervised driving with your teen. You never know until you ask.

CHAPTER 31

Tracking Your Teen

The best car safety device is a rearview mirror with a cop in it.
DUDLEY MOORE

Would you like to hand off the car keys to your teen, settle in for an evening at home, and be able to track exactly where he went, how long he stayed, who the passengers were in the car, what the conversations were about, and how fast he was going at all points along the trip? Of course you would. Well, now you can. Whether you choose to employ the technology to do this is another issue, but it's all possible today with a startling array of choices.

Data-recording devices have already been in many cars for quite a while. "Black boxes" or event data recorders (EDRs) were introduced in cars along with air bags beginning in the 1970s. Those early units recorded information when the air bag deployed, primarily vehicle deceleration and whether the driver seat belt was fastened. Today's models may record data including vehicle speed, seat-belt usage, braking, engine speed, and throttle position in the seconds before and after a crash.

What you may not realize is just how many cars contain data-recording devices today. NHTSA estimates that more than 30 million cars and trucks now on the road have black boxes, including more than three-quarters of all new vehicles. Global Positioning Systems such as OnStar capture additional data, including a continuous record of location and speed. (All this recorded information, by the way, is potentially available to insurers, rental companies, law-enforcement agencies, and assorted other governmental entities, but that's another subject entirely.)

New products using increasingly sophisticated technology can now record and track far more information about your vehicle's operation and occupants. In addition to these data-recording devices, we may soon see in-car camera systems that record for your viewing pleasure everything that goes on inside your car. The Mayo Clinic conducted a 26-week trial in 2004 with Minnesota high school students, in which tiny cameras were mounted on their rearview mirrors. Seat-belt use increased from 33 percent to virtually 100 percent during the study, and the near misses, hard braking, and swerves that triggered the cameras dropped from an average 24 incidents per week to nearly zero.

While it's never been easier to track your teen, the decision about whether to use one of these systems can be difficult. On the one hand, they can be very effective in curbing dangerous or irresponsible driving behavior. At the same time, building trust with your teen means giving him the opportunity, out from under your watchful eye, to earn that trust and to act responsibly. After all, our true character is revealed by what we do when nobody's looking.

Your teen may argue that such a device invades his privacy. You can legitimately take the stance that how he drives (especially with your car) isn't a private matter and that if he's driving responsibly, he shouldn't be concerned. For teens who have violated agreements about driving behavior or car use, a monitoring device can be very effective. But you have to decide how to balance the critical need to establish trust with your teen with the potential benefits of tracking technology, which may help keep your teen safer on the road.

There might be an easier way for you to deal with this without overstepping any bounds that make you uncomfortable. As noted earlier, whether you realize it or not, your car probably already has some form of installed data-recording device. If your or your teen's vehicle does, simply let him know that the car is equipped from the factory with technology that records data about how the car is operated. That's all you need to say. You can attribute the technology to Big Brother—the federal government, the auto industry, the CIA, the insurance cartel— and not his supersnoop parents. Let his fertile imagination work on the issue of whether you can or would access the information.

The use of any kind of monitoring device shouldn't be a secret to your teen. That's a guaranteed way to destroy trust. If you do decide you want to employ some kind of tracking system, have your teen be involved in choosing and buying it. Remind him that it can also be used to alert you when he's in trouble or the car is stolen. Monitoring systems can also give your teen a built-in excuse to drive more responsibly when he's with friends. Don't underestimate the significance of this point. Peer pressure can be exceptionally hard to resist for teens, and a monitoring device can make it much easier to brush off friends influencing him to speed or go somewhere he's not supposed to. His excuse can be that his parents will know, and he'll lose driving privileges.

Basic tracking systems record data on a device that you can unplug and connect to your computer, providing information about your vehicle's trips, which can include:

- Time and date.
- Distance traveled.
- Speed and idle time.
- Hard accelerations and decelerations.
- Engine diagnostic trouble codes.
- Audible alarms with user-set speed, acceleration, and braking limits.

Some systems can alert you when aggressive driving is detected by sending e-mails or text messages, flashing a dashboard light, or honking the car's horn, and others can even set "geo-fence" boundaries, alerting you if your car travels outside those boundaries.

More sophisticated versions are installed in cars and employ GPS technology, which adds the ability to monitor wherever your car is and how long it's been at any location. These systems typically offer real-time access via instant e-mail or a Web page, usually requiring monthly fees to transmit the data.

Although there are many products with a variety of brand names, most employ similar technology and are manufactured by just a few companies, including AirIQ Technologies, Advanced Tracking Technologies, CSI Wireless, and Discrete Wireless. Costs range from about $150 for a basic system without instant tracking to $400 or more plus monthly fees for systems incorporating GPS technology.

The following Web sites offer information on a variety of driver-monitoring systems:

> www.ADT.com
> www.alltrackusa.com
> www.davisnet.com
> www.directed.com
> www.drivediagnostics.com
> www.innosurance.com
> www.roadsafety.com
> www.safetytrac.com
> www.smart-driver.com
> www.teenarrivealive.com
> www.traveleyes.com

Check with your auto insurer, too. Insurance companies are beginning to show interest in the technology, and some have begun offering substantial discounts if you let them track your teen's driving patterns with a monitoring device.

If you want to go low-tech and inexpensive, consider bumper stickers. Check out www.tellmymom.com. For $55 a year, they'll send you a "How's My Driving?" bumper sticker with a toll-free number to report irresponsible driving behavior, which will trigger an e-mail or a phone call to you about the incident.

CHAPTER

32

The Checkered Flag

Adolescence is perhaps nature's way of preparing parents to welcome the empty nest.

KAREN SAVAGE AND PATRICIA ADAMS,
THE GOOD STEPMOTHER

For parents of teenagers, peace of mind is both rare and treasured. If you have a bit more of it the next time your teen pulls out of the driveway, this book has accomplished its purpose. You'll still worry. She'll still make mistakes and poor decisions. It's the birthright of a teen, as well as an essential element of her passage to adulthood.

But if you've spent time working through this book with her, helping her become more crashproof, she'll make far fewer mistakes when she drives. The odds are good that she will also be a better driving teacher to her own teens, your grandkids, so the care and love you've shown will echo for generations to come.

Although the focus has been on how to avoid the dangers of the road and keep your child safer, I hope that the time you've spent together has also given your teen a taste of the joy of driving, too. Wrapped in our shiny metal cocoons, we have the freedom to escape for a while, visit friends and family, travel to incredible places, and experience the joy of mastering a marvelous machine.

Don't underestimate the degree to which what you've been doing is actually teaching your teen how to *drive through life*. Think about it.

You've demonstrated that complex tasks require commitment, practice, and homework and that attention to detail pays off. You've shown her that by being thoughtful and respectful of herself, her passengers, and others on the road, she'll not only be safer but happier during the journey. It sounds to me like a pretty good metaphor for the daily conduct of her life.

As you work with your teen, you'll witness instances that will assure you that your messages are getting through. For me, one came while Brittany was driving on a warm, foggy night down a country road. The road was fringed with woods, from which deer would frequently emerge and launch themselves across the road, in their endearingly stupid and suicidal way. My wife and I had apparently drilled into her the proper way to deal with deer launching, because as soon as I uttered, "Remember there's a lot of deer in this area . . ." she finished with, "If one runs across the road, I'll brake, but not too hard. I won't swerve at all, and I'll hold tight onto the wheel, steering straight ahead."

We both laughed, and I felt more confident that if it happened, she'd react that way instinctively. For that particular driving situation, she was hardwired. She'd heard it (multiple times), said it verbally (reinforcing the audio), and actively visualized the sequence as she was talking about it. A month from now or three years from now, I'd like to believe her brain can't help but remember to instruct her hands and feet in that sequence before she can even think about it.

I'm sure that learning to drive while I was writing this book added to the pressure on her. Early on, I took a notebook with me when we drove together, occasionally jotting down ideas. She thought I was cataloguing her every driving move. No more notebook.

In addition to being somewhat of a guinea pig for me, she was also a source of material. When she'd make a driving mistake, she'd say, "Dad, you're not going to put this in the book, are you?" And I'd reply, "Of course not, honey." Then there'd be a little pause, and she'd say, "You're going to, aren't you, Dad?" And I'd say, "Of course I am, honey."

Since I had done the research, knew the statistics, and written the exercises, I was going to make sure she experienced every one of them. As a result, I had planned for the supervised driving period with her to last at least a year. That didn't mean continuous supervision for the whole time, but it meant supervised driving over a period that included all types of weather and driving situations, with her gaining more independence and ability to drive on her own as she earned it. If that took six months to a year after she got her license at 16, so be it.

I guess I assumed she would be thinking along the same lines, under the delusion that she understood and agreed with everything, as if she had helped me write the book or something. Wrong. She thought it was nice that Dad was writing a book and everything but pretty much assumed that when she turned 16, she'd be driving totally on her own. By this time, she had already accumulated at least 70 hours of supervised driving time with me and my wife, after all. In other words, I hadn't done as good a job of setting her expectations as I have advised you to do.

Several weeks before her sixteenth birthday, she mentioned how much she was looking forward to getting her license. I told her that it was exciting that she would be getting her license soon but reminded her that it didn't mean we were finished with our driving together.

A fair amount of wailing and gnashing of teeth ensued. Tears flowed.

"You don't trust me! You don't trust me enough to drive by myself!"

"That's not quite true. I trust you as a person. I just don't fully trust any 16-year-old I love with a couple of months' training to drive a gasoline-powered, 4,000-pound rocket around town."

More tears were followed by a long and generally positive discussion about how parenting sometimes means holding firm even when it would be easier, not to mention more peaceful, to cave in.

She understood, sort of, but still wasn't very happy.

I acknowledged her point of view and reiterated that we were still fated to spend many hours together in the car. Then I said that I was looking forward to it and was saddened that she didn't exactly seem thrilled about it.

More tears, different ones this time.

"I like being with you. I just don't like it when you yell at me. I feel as if I'm under constant scrutiny when you're in the car."

"Constant scrutiny is the point, isn't it? The last thing I want to do is make you uncomfortable, though. And as for yelling, I can only remember yelling three times, and each time it was necessary and in fact saved us and a bunch of others from disaster."

"That's not true! Well, maybe I didn't brake in time that once and turned in front of traffic that other time."

"Look, you're doing great. I trust you. But we've got more work to do. Are you ready to drive in downtown Chicago during an earthquake or a tsunami?"

"I don't plan on driving in downtown Chicago during an earthquake! And we don't have tsunamis on Lake Michigan."

"Maybe not, but wouldn't you like to be able to drive by yourself in downtown Chicago sometime?"

"Well, yeah."

"Are you confident you're ready to do that now?"

"No way."

"That's what I'm talking about. You still need me."

"You're a pain."

"I know. I'll make sure we finish this before your junior year of college, OK? Let's go drive."

And so we did. In the rain.

APPENDIX

STATES' REQUIREMENTS FOR YOUNG DRIVERS

STATE	MINIMUM HOURS PARENTAL SUPERVISION	SUPERVISION FOR AT LEAST 6 MONTHS	RESTRICTIONS ON UNSUPERVISED NIGHT DRIVING	LIMITS ON TEEN PASSENGERS
ALABAMA	30	X	X	X
ALASKA	40	X	X	X
ARIZONA	25			
ARKANSAS	None	X		
CALIFORNIA	50	X	X	X
COLORADO	50	X	X	X
CONNECTICUT	20	X	X	X
DELAWARE	None	X	X	X
D.C.	50	X	X	X
FLORIDA	50	X	X	
GEORGIA	40	X	X	X
HAWAII	None	X	X	X
IDAHO	50		X	
ILLINOIS	25		X	X
INDIANA	None		X	X
IOWA	20	X	X	
KANSAS	50			
KENTUCKY	None	X		
LOUISIANA	None	X	X	

STATES' REQUIREMENTS FOR YOUNG DRIVERS

STATE	MINIMUM HOURS PARENTAL SUPERVISION	SUPERVISION FOR AT LEAST 6 MONTHS	RESTRICTIONS ON UNSUPERVISED NIGHT DRIVING	LIMITS ON TEEN PASSENGERS
MAINE	35	X	X	X
MARYLAND	60	X	X	
MASSACHUSETTS	12	X	X	X
MICHIGAN	50	X	X	
MINNESOTA	30	X		
MISSISSIPPI	None	X	X	
MISSOURI	20	X	X	
MONTANA	50	X	X	X
NEBRASKA	50		X	
NEVADA	50	X	X	X
NEW HAMPSHIRE	20		X	X
NEW JERSEY	None	X	X	X
NEW MEXICO	50	X	X	X
NEW YORK	20	X	X	X
NORTH CAROLINA	None	X	X	X
NORTH DAKOTA	None	X		
OHIO	50	X	X	
OKLAHOMA	40	X	X	X
OREGON	50	X	X	X
PENNSYLVANIA	50	X	X	
RHODE ISLAND	50	X	X	X
SOUTH CAROLINA	40	X	X	X

STATES' REQUIREMENTS FOR YOUNG DRIVERS

STATE	MINIMUM HOURS PARENTAL SUPERVISION	SUPERVISION FOR AT LEAST 6 MONTHS	RESTRICTIONS ON UNSUPERVISED NIGHT DRIVING	LIMITS ON TEEN PASSENGERS
SOUTH DAKOTA	None	X	X	
TENNESSEE	50	X	X	X
TEXAS	None	X	X	X
UTAH	40		X	X
VERMONT	40	X		X
VIRGINIA	40	X	X	X
WASHINGTON	50	X	X	X
WEST VIRGINIA	30	X	X	X
WISCONSIN	30	X	X	X
WYOMING	50	X	X	X

Sources: Insurance Institute for Highway Safety, as of October 2005; Advocates for Highway and Auto Safety, October 2004. Additional and updated information available at www.iihs.org.

DRUGS AND INTOXICANTS AND THEIR EFFECTS ON DRIVING

TYPE OF DRUG	DRUG EFFECT	POSSIBLE DRIVING BEHAVIOR/HAZARD
DEPRESSANTS		
BARBITURATES **TRANQUILIZERS** **ALCOHOL** **ANTIHISTAMINES** **METHOAQUALONE**	Drowsiness Reduced alertness Slow reactions Intense emotion Impaired judgment Loss of concentration Dizziness Reduced coordination	Inconsistent driving speeds Inappropriate honking Hard weaving Driving too close to shoulders Driving without headlights
CANNABIS		
MARIJUANA, HASHISH	Slow reactions Difficulty concentrating Depth-perception distortion Reduced short-term memory Altered sense of time and space	Jerky starts and stops Tailgating Passing without enough room Disregarding traffic control
STIMULANTS		
AMPHETAMINES **DIET PILLS** **COCAINE** **CAFFEINE** **NICOTINE** **METHAMPHETAMINE** **RITALIN**	Impatient/impulsive behavior Aggressive/hostile behavior Overactive and excited Less coordination Irritability Reduced concentration	Running red lights Tailgating Unreasonably fast or slow speed Hard weaving Honking or flashing lights

DRUGS AND INTOXICANTS AND THEIR EFFECTS ON DRIVING

TYPE OF DRUG	DRUG EFFECT	POSSIBLE DRIVING BEHAVIOR/HAZARD
INHALANTS		
SOLVENTS (GLUE)	Visual hallucinations	Running red lights
GASES (WHIPPITTS)	Severe mood swings	Tailgating
NITRITES (POPPERS)	Violent behavior Loss of coordination Hearing loss Limb spasms	Giving obscene gestures Cutting off drivers Entering intersections improperly
NARCOTICS		
HEROIN	Sight impaired	Speeding
CODEINE	Slow reaction time	Failure to dim headlights
OPIUM	Motor skills impaired	Driving too slow
MORPHINE	Difficulty concentrating	Riding the brakes
METHADONE	Restlessness	
HALLUCINOGENS		
LSD	Hallucinations	Giving obscene gestures
PEYOTE	Confusion and suspicion	Tailgating
PCP	Time and distance distortion	Disregarding traffic controls
MESCALINE	Slow reaction Lack of coordination Forgetfulness Rapid mood swings Violent behavior	Riding the brakes

USEFUL ORGANIZATIONS

Advocates for Auto and Highway Safety, 750 First St., NE, Ste 901, Washington DC 20002; (202) 408-1711; *www.saferoads.org*. A coalition of insurers, citizens' groups, and public health and safety organizations.

American Driver & Traffic Safety Education Association, Highway Safety Center, Indiana University of Pennsylvania, R & P Bldg, Indiana, PA 15705; (724) 357-3975; *www.adtsea.org*. Works with driver's education instructors and state authorities to improve driver's education standards and practices.

Drivetrain, Inc. 1292 Willowhaven Drive, San Jose, CA 95126; (408) 832-3566; *www.drivetrainusa.com*. Drivetrain offers innovative courses in advanced driving at several locations in the U.S., featuring internationally trained instructors dedicated to taking teens and adults beyond basic driver education.

Driving Skills for Life, (888) 987-8765; *www.drivingskillsforlife.com*. Sponsored by the Ford Motor Company and the Governors Highway Safety Association, this site provides learning material for safe driving for use by students, parents, educators, and instructors for use at home, in school, and in community settings.

Insurance Institute for Highway Safety, 1005 N. Glebe Rd., Ste 800, Arlington VA 22201; (703) 247-1500; *www.iihs.org*. Researches highway safety and conducts crash tests on new cars and trucks; funded by auto insurance companies.

Mothers Against Drunk Driving, P.O. Box 541699, Dallas, TX 75354-1688; (800) GET-MADD; *www.madd.org.* With more than 600 chapters nationwide, fights drunken driving and supports victims of alcohol-related crimes.

National Highway Traffic Safety Administration, 400 Seventh St., SW, Washington DC, 20590; (202) 366-9550; *www.nhtsa.dot.gov.* Issues vehicle safety standards, investigates safety defects, and orders recalls when necessary.

National Safety Council, 1121 Spring Lake Dr, Itasca, IL 60143; (630) 285-1121; *www.nsc.org.* Conducts research and provides information on highway safety.

RoadReadyTeens, *www.roadreadyteens.org.* An online safety program for parents and teens sponsored by several corporate and non-profit safety groups.

Safe Smart Women 1201 Noyes Drive, Silver Spring, MD 20910; (410) 562-1008; *www.s2w.org.* This nonprofit group provides free clinics in various cities for female drivers, covering safety, maintenance, and driving behavior.

Students Against Destructive Decisions, PO BOX 800, Marlborough, MA 01752; (877) SADD-INC; *www.sadd.org.* A peer-to-peer education organization with 10,000 chapters in middle and high schools.

Top Driver, Inc. 1141 Arlington Heights Road, Suite D, Arlington Heights, IL 60005; (800) 374-8373; *www.topdriver.com.* With locations in many states, Top Driver sets the standard for commercial driver education schools, with consistent, high-quality training programs.

Courtesy CQ Researcher

ACKNOWLEDGMENTS

I owe a debt of gratitude to many individuals and organizations whose contributions were essential to this book.

The National Safety Council, the Insurance Institute for Highway Safety, the American Driver and Traffic Safety Education Association, and the National Highway Traffic Safety Administration, among others, provided crucial data and statistics on which many of the driving strategies and exercises were based.

Invaluable training, information, quotes, and manuscript review were provided by numerous experts, professional driving instructors, and organizations, notably Larry Costain, Bob Green, Jeff Payne, John Raffa, Ron Jones, Sam Horn, Gordon Booth, Kristin Backstrom, Dr. Owen Crabb, Dave Long, Eddie Wren, Ivars Bergs, Debbie Cottonware, Ray Shallwani, Excel Driving School, Trish Johnson and Top Driver, Inc., and the Skip Barber School of Racing. The advice, anecdotes, and reality checks offered by so many parents and teens were also much appreciated.

I am most fortunate to have Ed Knappman of New England Publishing Associates as my agent, Meghan Stevenson as editorial assistant, and especially Cherise Davis of Simon & Schuster as my editor. All are dedicated, consummate professionals who have been instrumental in making this book a reality.

Finally, thank you, Sherri—my wife, partner, best friend, chief supporter, and co-pilot in negotiating the twists and turns of being a parent.

INDEX